To my mother Constance Carroll Brahm

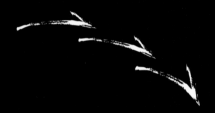

Who took me to the Museum of Natural History,
told me about far-away places
and encouraged me to find them.

The Himalayan Trilogy expeditions received the
National Geographic Air and Water Conservation
Fund award in 2016 for raising awareness of
anthropomorphic climate change.

CONVERSATIONS
WITH
SACRED
MOUNTAINS

A Journey Along
Yunnan's Tea Caravan Trail

Laurence Brahm

IBIS
IBIS PRESS
Lake Worth, FL

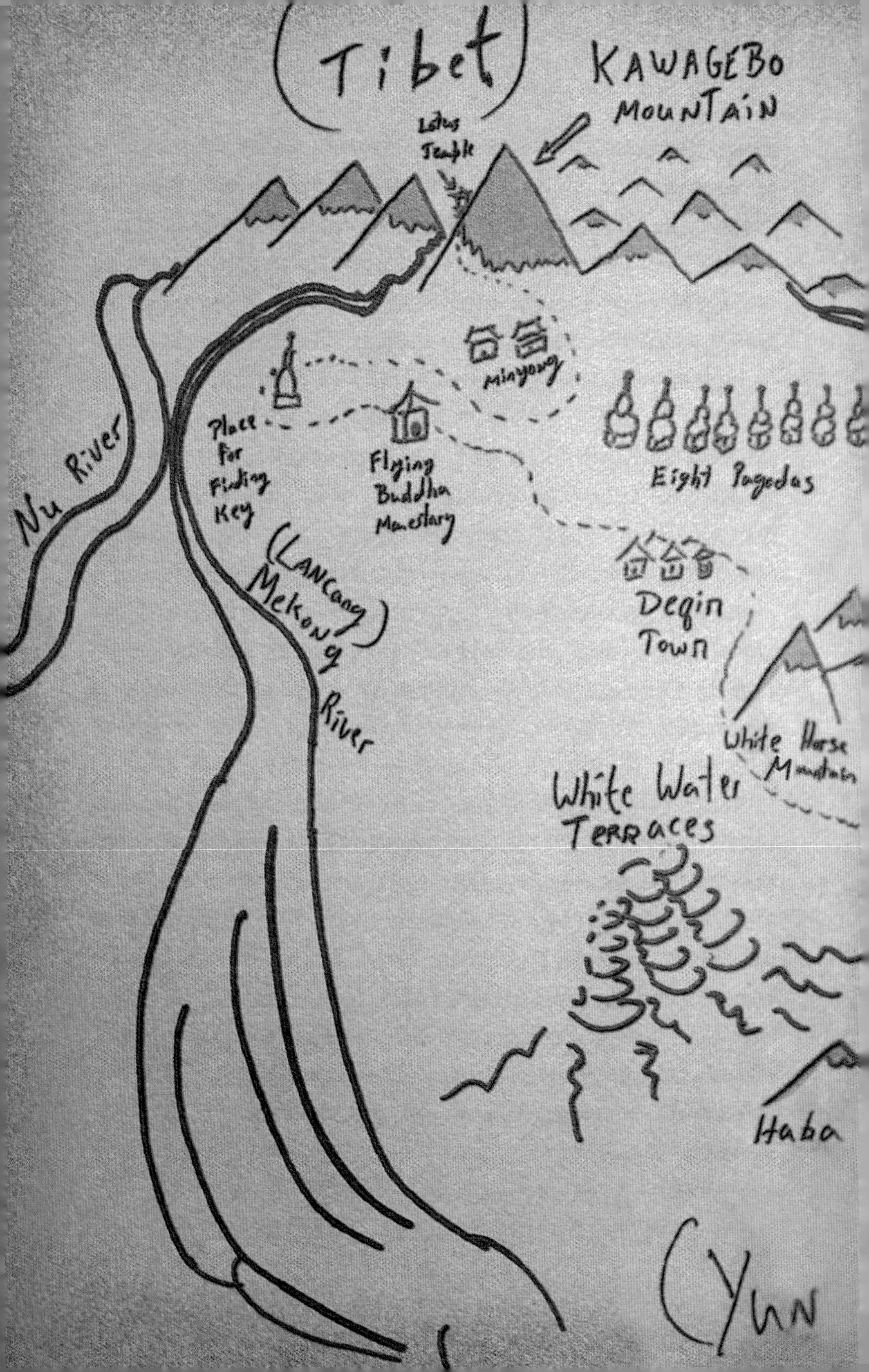

(Tibet)

KAWAGEBO
MOUNTAIN

Lotus
Temple

合合
Minyong

Nu River

Place
for
Finding
Key

Flying
Buddha
Monestary

合合合合合合合
Eight Pagodas

(LANcang)
Mekong
River

合合合
Deqin
Town

White Horse
Mountain

White Water
Terraces

Haba

(Yun

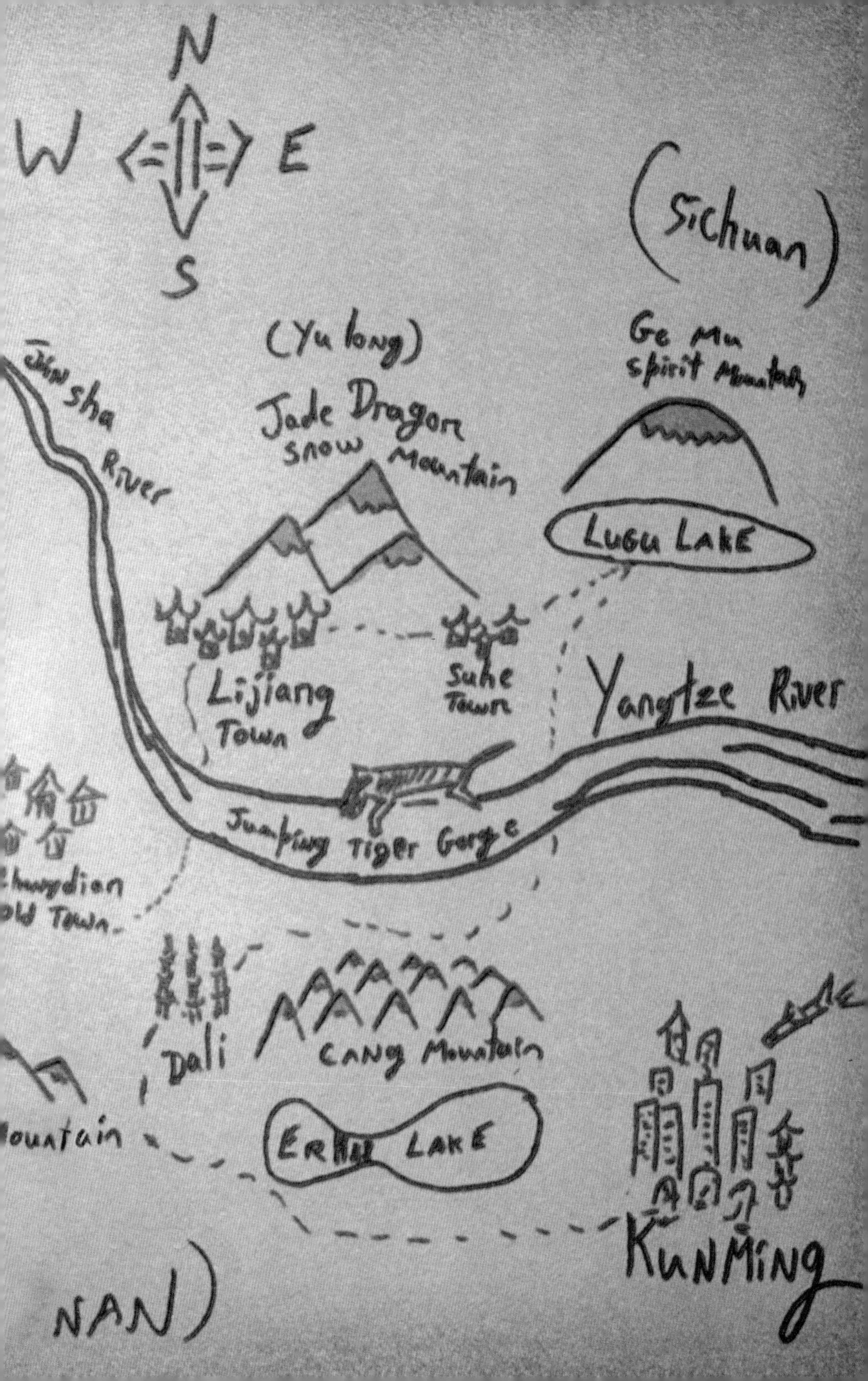

N
W
E
S
(Sichuan)
(Yulong)
Jade Dragon Snow Mountain
Ge Mu spirit Mountain
Lugu Lake
Jinsha River
Lijiang Town
Suhe Town
Yangtze River
Jumping Tiger Gorge
Zhongdian Old Town
Dali
Cang Mountain
Erhai Lake
ountain
Kunming
NAN)

"Though he went outside long ago, the valley of Blue Moon remembers him still."

—*Lost Horizon*

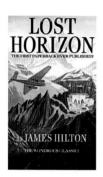

James HIlton's 1933 novel "Lost Horizons" depicts a Himalayan realm of holistic values in the mystical "Valley of the Blue Moon." There, man respects his environment which in turn protects mankind. Ever since Hilton's novel, people have been searching for Shangri-la. For some reason, it cannot be found.

Starting in 2002, tired of the crass commercialism and money worship that saturated every aspect of life in Beijing, I left my career as an investment lawyer in China. I closed my boutique investment consulting firm, introduced the clients to my lawyer and banker friends, hung up my suit and tie, and dug up old hiking books and a backpack that had been forgotten. Inspired by Hilton's vision of finding such a place as Shangri-la, I launched three expeditions to search for it. This three year journey became a trilogy of three books and subsequent documentary films:"Searching for Shangri-la" (2002), "Conversations with Sacred Mountains" (2003), and "Shambhala Sutra" (2004). Each documents a different expedition respectively during those years.

"Conversations with Sacred Mountains" chronicles my 2003 journey for which Hilton's novel "Lost Horizon" served literally as my guidebook. The actual route taken, followed the ancient "Tea Caravan Trail" in Yunnan Province. This was the only known route into Tibetan areas from Southwest China in 1933. The ethnic groups and their different cultures, together with the geography, most likely provided actual reference points that Hilton drew upon from National Geographic reports at the time, in creating his fictional account of Shangri-la.

I began the journey in Kunming, the capital of Yunnan Province. The route followed: Dali, once ancient kingdom of the Bai nationality; to Lijiang, the kingdom of the Naxi nationality (who still have the oldest living pictural language in the world); through Yi nationality villages who still practice "slash and burn" (the oldest form of agriculture); on to isolated Lugu Lake, home to the matriarchal Mosu nation of women, and finally to Zhongdian and Deqin in Shangrila County, where Tibetans revere the sacred Kawegabo Mountain.

I retraced this route several times in the years that followed. During each visit I was struck by the tidal wave of encroaching commercialization. In contrast stood the local people from each of these ethnic nationalities, determined to adhere to their traditions and culture. However, in the end, practically speaking, cultural preservation depended on economics. All along the Tea Caravan Trail, each ethnic group adopted small scale businesses. From eco-tourism, tea house lodging, to craft revitalization, organic agriculture and harvesting – these all became platforms to sustain their way of life and the traditions they hold dear. They were finding a middle way. It was pragmatic idealism. The origin of social enterprise.

People living on the Himalayan plateau possess within their traditions a rich vestige of knowledge on managing delicate bio-diversity. That knowledge can teach us how to live our lives in a more holistic way. Protecting our environment, in turn ensures our own survival. This was the whole point of Hilton's book, written little less than a century ago. Maybe the Hollywood movie version missed the point. Legends from Kawegabo Mountain are revealed in the last section of this book. These parables contain a set of local teachings. In a modern context they could be understood as a crash course in envrionmental protection and sustainable development.

Today, in Yunnan Province one can find some of China's most pioneering programs for sustainable development and social enterprise. I found inspiration from the many people met in the course of my journeys there. The overeaching concept of Himalayan Consensus (www. himalayanconsensus.org) arose from their experiences.

The title "Coversations with Sacred Mountains" reflects the idea that our own survival as human species depends on how well we take care of our environment. Each ethnic group visited along the Tea Caravan Trail has its own sacred mountain. That mountain as a protector spirit assures survival of their nationality. Given the delicate biodiversity of the Himalayan plateau, traditional reverence for the mountain established pragmatic rules for environmental protection and each ethnic group's careful and balanced use of the natural resources available to them. In short, the different ethnic groups of Yunnan were practicing "sustainable development" long before we ever thought of this idea. Today we should learn from them.

Contents

ZHONGDIAN

KAWAGEBO

"Tears of a Nomad"

They will cover sacred mountains with cable cars

They will turn ethnic dances into freak shows

They will trade nationality clothes for brand names

They will laugh at your culture buying souveniers made in
their factories

They will bulldoze your architecture constructing
shopping malls

They will destroy the symbols and images that connect
us to the universe

They will bury your happiness for GDP

Because they worship only money

And then they will tell you, that they are the ones who
are civilized.

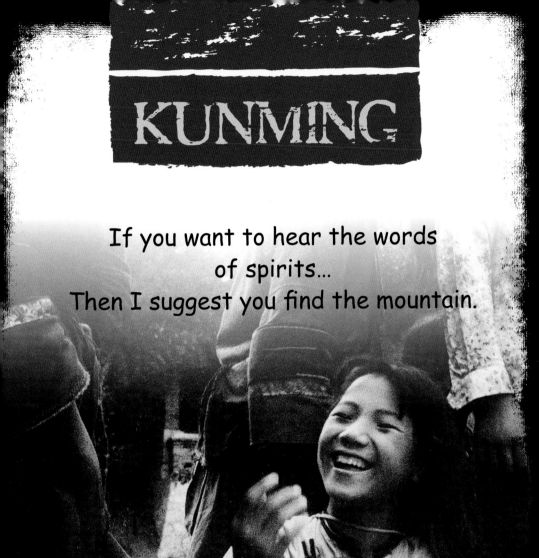

KUNMING

If you want to hear the words
of spirits...
Then I suggest you find the mountain.

Kunming is the capital of Yunnan Province. The airplanes from Beijing arrive here. The airport reminds me of Bangkok, which all goes to show that this is probably the only province in China that has gotten its act together on tourism. This is because the people of Yunnan look south to Thailand and Southeast Asia for their inspiration. Less influenced by Beijing, they try a different approach here.

Of course, there is nothing new about this. In ancient times, Chinese emperors banished rebels to Yunnan. In those days, Yunnan was considered the furthest border of the Chinese empire, inhabited by hill tribes locked in by mountains and valleys and who clung on to their cultures. As for those rebels banished there by the emperors, they learned to survive in the hills from the tribes.

When I first visited Kunming over 20 years ago, it was a charming city of old wooden and gray brick buildings tottering along canals in leafy tree-lined streets. Now all the old buildings are gone and the trees have been uprooted. It is a so-called modern city consisting of lots of cement and glass. The city charm was obliterated for the international flower exhibition years ago and the local government thought it would be very international to destroy everything relating to the natural environment of their city by covering all the flowers with cement. So when you arrive in Kunming, it looks like any other Chinese city. But it is the starting point of any journey in Yunnan. One must begin the journey by leaving the city.

Kunming has become a kind of rock-and-roll town. Factories along the old canals have been converted into studio lofts, where a number of creative artists work between the seasons. Like travelers, these artists really use the city as a stepping-off point to other places along the Tea Caravan Trail.

The Tea Caravan Trail literally runs north to south from Simao and Pu'er, Yunnan's rich tea-producing soil valleys. One route cuts south through the Red River Valley, extending to Vietnam, Laos and Myanmar. The second and main route runs to Dali, Lijiang, the Lugu Lake, Zhongdian, and overland past sacred Kawagebo Mountain to the holy city of Lhasa. From there it veers off to Shigatze, then to Nepal and India.

Crossing the Tea Caravan Trail, tea was brought to India, and in turn the pony caravans brought Buddhist sutras back to China. It was through the Tea Caravan Trail (sometimes referred to as the "Southern Silk Road") that a commodities, ideas, and philosophy synergized into a confluence of culture between East, South and Southeast Asia.

In ancient times, light-footed mule and pony caravans treked along this train.Tightly woven baskets of tea compressed to look like bricks, were piled on their backs. The ponies had special saddles which allowed for packing vast quantities of these tea bricks. The journey was arduous and trecherous. Along the way, different ethnic groups each had their own station on the Tea Caravan Trail. So a journey to bring tea to India, meant traversing across different tribal worlds and passing through the realms of their beliefs.

At each stop along the Tea Caravan Trail, local people had their own sacred mountain. They worshiped the spirits of the mountain, which in turn protected them. Another way of explaining this, is to understand their relationship with the natural environment as one of awe and respect. By caring for their environment and the sources of water and food that it provided, nature in turn took care of them. They observed the unspoken rules of nature. When flowers opened in the spring, melting mountain glaciers nurtured their fields and grasslands. Hand-hewn canals served as conduits from the mountains through villages and towns bringing crystal fresh water, and their civilzation flourished.

Yes, the people never forgot their shamans and lamas, who in turn always remembered to have a conversation with a sacred mountain. I went to find those shamans and lamas. In turn they taught me how to have a conversation with a sacred mountain.

This is the story of my 2003 expedition hiking along the Tea Caravan Trail. I travelled from Kunming to Dali, home of the Bai people. Then to Lijiang, kingdom of the ancient Naxi people who still have the oldest continuing hyroglyphic language in the world. Then on to Lugu Lake, home of the Mosu nation of women. Passing Yi mountain tribe villages still practicing slash and burn agriculture. Traversing on to Shangri-la country and ending the journey in pilgrimage to Kawegabo, the protector mountain revered by Tibetans.

At these stops along the Tea Caravan Trail, I found that each people honor their own sacred mountain. This story is about following the trail, and learning from them, how to have a conversation with the mountains.

Sampling Disillusionment

"Cigars had burned low, and we were beginning to sample the disillusionment...I got a short note...to say he was off on his wanderings again and would have no settled address for some months. He was going to Kashmir, he wrote and hence 'east.' I was not surprised."

—*Lost Horizon*

I was born in New York City. I guess you could say I grew up in New York City. I lived there until I was ten years old. Then I moved to Connecticut.

One of my earliest memories was of sitting on the carpeted floor of our New York apartment, leafing through National Geographic. I was just a little boy. I was so fascinated by the photos — I could not stop looking at them. What fascinated me most were those pictures of laughing children, women with colorful bandannas wrapped around their heads, tribal headdresses of dangling old silver coins, and timber houses precariously built on stilts somewhere in Asia, tucked in misty valleys, propped on mountainsides. Somehow I wanted to go to these places and stay in one of those houses.

These places seemed far away. Sometimes, I caught glimpses of them on the 5 p.m. evening news with Walter Cronkite. Green Berets patrolling villages. I could see them sometimes in the scratchy footage, pushing through brush. I did not understand why so many soldiers wanted to blow up those timber houses on stilts. People told me it was to save the women and children wearing bandannas.

I remember, as a child, wandering through the Museum of Natural History in New York, dwarfed by huge dinosaur bones, big feet, stuffed bears and stuffed Tibetan antelope. I seemed to stare for hours at a long American Indian canoe. There were exhibits of manikins dressed in bearskins and wearing shaman masks, the force of which filled the entire room. I would stare up at the shaman masks for what seemed like hours.

The museum fascinated me. Cavernous corridors led into rooms with more manikins in traditional costumes — Eskimo, African, Arab, and Polynesian. As a young boy, I stared at the manikins, wondering what life was like for people in these places who really wore these clothes. Then one day, the museum opened its Asian room. I went to see it.

The hill tribe images returned. I could not get them out of my mind. Once again, I wondered what it would be like to live in a timber house on a mountainside with nothing else around, except poppy flowers floating in the wind and the sound of one's own echo dreamily calling out from within the depths of a chasm cut through terraced fields by a river flowing from melting glaciers in mountains that can never be climbed. I thought about climbing the mountains.

That was when I moved to Connecticut.

I took a course in high school on India and Southeast Asia. Interesting how two enormous land and cultural masses encompassing

many millennium of history could be compressed into a single half semester class and taught to American high school students as "India and Southeast Asia". It sounded like something a cheerleader would say at a football match.

The autumn leaves fell one by one across my feet at a football match. I had forgotten about the teams and could not hear the cheerleaders anymore. My eyes were following the leaves, drifting with the wind that somehow came from far off mountains. My mind was already in the mountains. Then I thought about "India and Southeast Asia."

What they forgot to teach us in class was that the source of these powerful cultures is three great and powerful rivers — the Ganges, the

Mekong, and the Yangtze. These rivers meet before a sacred Tibetan snow mountain which cannot be climbed. After listening to a few more lectures, I began to look for the old National Geographic magazines. I was looking for the mountains, and for the people who live on the sides of the mountain.

I found them. In fact, I found a map tucked inside one old copy of National Geographic, illustrating where all of the hill tribes of continental Southeast Asia are — Vietnam, Cambodia, Burma, Thailand, and a Chinese province called Yunnan. I had never heard of Yunnan before. It was not on the Walter Cronkite news reports. There were romantic illustrations of the Miao, Dai, Yi, and Long Neck Karen. They lived in timber houses on stilts propped on hillsides. They wore bandannas.

I remember unfolding the old map and using scotch tape to paste it on the wall over my desk where I did my homework. I told my mom I was going to memorize all the names of the tribes. I did. Then one day, I forgot about the map, and the tribes. I left it pasted on the white plaster wall in my childhood bedroom. I had already left.

I arrived in China in 1981 as a student. Everyone was wearing green and blue. I did not see any of the colorful hill tribe costumes that I had seen in National Geographic. All I saw were some dreary-eyed Tibetans hanging out at Beijing's railroad station. And lots of other dreary-eyed Chinese sitting on over-stuffed blue and green canvas bags, sleeping on the bags, waiting for a train ticket back to somewhere where they had not come from too long ago or would not be in a hurry to go back to again. Why were they all waiting for a train ticket? I soon learnt that, in those days, even to buy a train ticket in China, one had to use guanxi or connections.

When I left China at the end of 1981, I went to Hong Kong.

In those days, Hong Kong seemed like the center of everything. Indeed, it was the center of China business. Business was the center of life. Everybody talked all day long about business. Yes, I forgot about the hill tribes in their steamy mountainside timber cabins on stilts. That all faded in my mind under the intensity of contract negotiations and the shrill of deal making, market runs and currency fluctuations on the open, forward, spot markets — to be discussed over coffee in the

morning, tea in the afternoon, and drinks at night in the bars, and then in the clubs until early morning.

During the 1980s, I worked as a lawyer writing contracts for multinationals investing in China. I worked for a British law firm in Hong Kong, wore a black suit, a blue shirt with a white collar and cufflinks. I dressed like this every day. Sometimes, I felt as if I could not breathe — stuffed into this suit that was stuffed into elevators stuffed with people going up through floors and floors and layers and layers of photocopied documents in skyscrapers of photocopies reaching to the sky. I would ride up and down the elevators every day. At night, I would dream of the photocopies.

PLEASE
DON'T
FEED
DINASAUR

That was the life of a lawyer specializing in China trade in Hong Kong during the 1980s. Actually, none of the so-called "China experts" really understood what was happening in China in those days. But that was not the point. Neither did anybody else. So it was quite sufficient to ride up and down the elevators of prestigious central financial district luxury office towers and talk about things that you really did not understand. For lawyers, accountants, consultants and night club hostesses, everything discussed was billable by the hour anyways, and priced relatively in accordance with the real estate printed on the address of the name card, which you presented to potential clients with both hands and a slight bow.

When it came time to leave the office and go on vacations, most of my lawyer colleagues would hit the beaches and bars in Manila, Phuket, Pattaya, or play golf. Golf was extremely important to lawyers, bankers and their clients. They would whittle away enormous amounts of time trying to fit little balls into slightly larger holes using instruments totally unsuitable for the task. I never joined these golf vacations.In fact, I felt the golf courses should all be nationalized and turned into organic crop communes to grow food for the poor!

Instead of learning to play golf, I went to those hill tribe areas to hike. I was looking for timber houses on stilts, leaning on hillsides in misty valleys beside mountains which could not be climbed. I trekked through poppy fields in northern Thailand, found the Hani and the Yi tribes living in timber houses on stilts, wearing colorful headdresses made of old silver coins. They were just like the ones I used to look at in National Geographic. I began to photograph them. I kept taking pictures, just like the ones in National Geographic.

To my surprise, these tribes had something in common. They all spoke the Yunnan dialect of Chinese. The tribal elders explained, once upon a time, they came from Yunnan, a province of China, a place called "south of the clouds". It was a place of sacred mountains connected by a trail that used to be the caravan route for tea which they grew on mountainsides beside their timber houses on stilts, until they were driven out to Thailand during the years of civil war, where they stayed and grew opium. The tea went, by horse, following a route connecting one sacred mountain with another, eventually reaching Lhasa. The story confused me and I really did not understand. I was too busy taking pictures.

I brought in my backpack some magic tricks, and performed them at night sitting by the hearth. The Hani and Yi were fascinated. Convinced I was a witch doctor, women brought me sick children, asking for cures. I only had asprin and some lomytol in my backpack. Breaking these into small pieces, I handed them to the women who gave them to their children. This disturbing incident taught me the need to bring medical facilities -regardless of how simple - to people in villages. Both rural and urban communities need these facillities. Somehow this encounter influenced me very deeply. Twenty years later I would set up medical clinics in Tibetan regions of western China. In some cases just having running water can prevent disease.

That night sitting by the hearth performing my magic tricks, the men of the village brought old guns and asked me if my magic could ward off bullets from their black powder hunting muskets. I confessed that I was not a witch doctor, and that these were only illussions. They asked me, what was an illusion.

The hill tribe infatuation kept me trekking. From hiking the Himalayan foothills of Nepal to jungles of Malaysia, I took a canoe up river looking for headhunters. Going from one Malaysian Chinese river trader's home to another, I made my way into the Borneo interior, finally finding longhouses of hunters who once hunted heads. I wanted to see the heads. Sure enough, skulls of Japanese soldiers taken in World War II hung from the center of a lodge. I slept in the lodge, under the heads. In the morning, I took more pictures.

Then I trekked through Nepal, Laos, Vietnam, Myanmar, visiting the hill tribes — Hani, Yi, Miao, Karen, and Hmong. After all of these trips — trekking and photographing — I would end up with the lawyers, bankers and businessmen talking over cigars at the Mandarin Hotel or Foreign Correspondents Club in Hong Kong. Over lobby lounge music, cigars and after-work drinks, I would show them pictures of the Borneo skulls, the Burmese Long Necks, and Lao women weaving along the Mekong. They showed me pictures of girls they picked up at the bars in

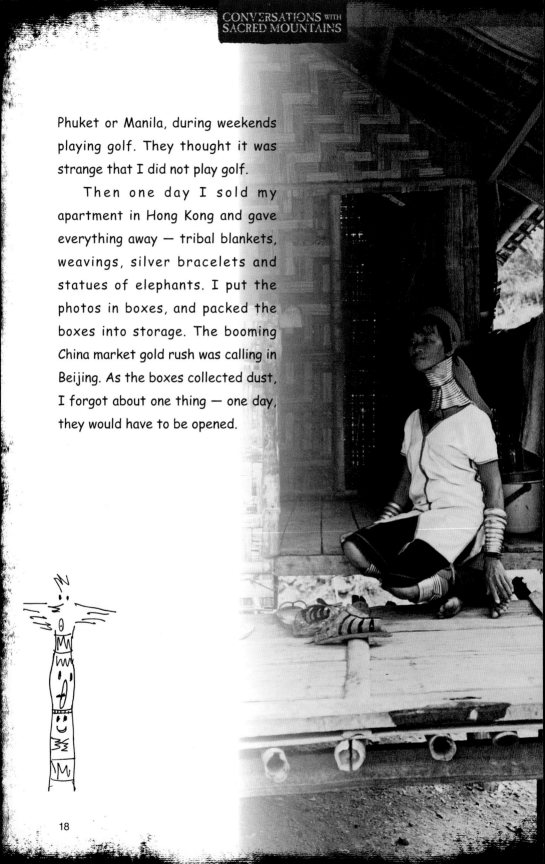

Phuket or Manila, during weekends playing golf. They thought it was strange that I did not play golf.

Then one day I sold my apartment in Hong Kong and gave everything away — tribal blankets, weavings, silver bracelets and statues of elephants. I put the photos in boxes, and packed the boxes into storage. The booming China market gold rush was calling in Beijing. As the boxes collected dust, I forgot about one thing — one day, they would have to be opened.

A Peacock

"She had the long, slender nose, high cheekbones, and egg pallor of the Manchu; her black hair was drawn tightly back and braided; she looked very finished and miniature. Her mouth was like a pink convolvulus, and she was quite still, except for her long-fingered hands."

—Lost Horizon

I first saw Yang Liping in Yunnan in the very early 1990s. I believe it was 1991. Her "Peacock Dance", mimicking a peacock, was both shocking and beautiful. I was stunned and mesmerized watching her live performance in Xishuangbanna, sitting together with a delegation of central bank officials from Beijing.

I had traveled to Yunnan as a legal advisor to a team of officials from the People's Bank of China to research and draft a law for negotiable instruments in China. Monetary policy had become my specialization after advising the central banks of Laos and Vietnam. The delegation had chosen to meet in Kunming and then Xishuangbanna, the home of ethnic Dai tribes, who are a lot like the Lao. After discussing regulatory restrictions for the manipulation of money, I slipped out the back door of our hotel, rented a jeep, and drove off into the hills looking for the Dai. I found them living in cramped villages built on stilts along misty rivers beside lonely white pagodas.

I saw Yang Liping again in 1992, this time on television. I was sitting in a dirty, run-down Sichuan restaurant in Lhasa, eating spicy toufu. The tiny television in a corner of the restaurant showed her performing the Peacock Dance for an audience that included some of China's heavyweight leaders. Somehow the last thing on my mind was the remote possibility that there would one day be a connection between myself, Tibetan Buddhism and Yang Liping. Somehow that was the last thing that could possibly have entered my mind that night while eating spicy toufu in a filthy Sichuan restaurant in Lhasa. I thought about it no more. I left Lhasa. It would be exactly ten years before I returned.

A decade later, I came across Yang Liping again in Kunming, where she had established a dance studio for sustaining the culture of ethnic minorities in Yunnan. As much of their dance and music is part of their oral tradition, rapid change and development were eroding their culture faster than it could be protected. Every road that opened to a village brought with it development and change, and Yang Liping was determined to save what she could while it was still there. To enable preservation of her people's culture on a sustainable basis, she brought young village children to her studio in Kunming, recorded their songs and filmed their dance. To keep their culture alive, she brought their different traditional dances and music into an ongoing performing arts program.

As I sat beside her, Yang Liping pointed to the girls dancing in synchronic rhythm. There was something totally organic about their movements. Their clothes and exquisite headdresses were woven in villages, maybe a generation or two before, passed from grandmother to mother to daughter. Their movements were natural, overflowing with a spirit that could not be choreographed.

Moving her long thin fingers in a slow movement like a Bodhisattva's mudra, Yang Liping pointed a finger — extended into the infinity of a single fingernail prolonged into a moment that seemed to hang in the air as if floating — toward the children as they danced. She whispered, "The children of Yunnan are pure; they are like little Buddhas."

I was momentarily struck by profundity, held in the simplicity of her words. In fact, I was totally taken back. Still craving for re-confirmation, I asked Yang Liping to repeat what she said.

She did not, just shrugged, and added, "The people of Yunnan are like that." As far as she was concerned, what was said should be understood. Otherwise, it was not meant to be understood. Then her fingers unfolded again like a fan and her eyes beamed with a depth of penetrating black as she talked about Yunnan and the ethnic minorities — her own people. "Xishuangbanna, in our tropical south, is home to the Dai people. It is their place locked in rice-terraced valleys along the

Mekong River. They are like the Thai and move in long sarongs of silk. Further along the Red River, which flows to Vietnam, is the place of the Wah. Some of their lifestyle and religious practices even resemble those in Africa. They pray to the sun. They live close to the sun. This way is right. Then there are the Yi people who are different. They live in mountains, slash and burn, and move when there is nothing left to keep them. They pray to fire and tigers and have no possessions because they do not stay long enough in one place to make possessions worth keeping."

"What about yourself?" I asked. "What ethnic group do you come from?"

"I am a Bai. Our home is Dali. It was once a kingdom. The old city is still well protected. Many artists are going there to find Shangri-La. It is the first stop on the Tea Caravan Trail. If you want to find Shangri-La, then maybe this is where you should begin your journey."

Then with a faint voice bordering on a slight gasp, Yang Liping talked about her home. "The lake, Erhai, is shaped like a Buddha's ear and reflects the Cang Mountain. But there is more than the scenery for you to discover in Dali. There, you will find the people and their culture intact. So it is a special place. I remember when I was young, we went into the water of the lake. Fish would swim between our legs — humanity and nature was in harmony. The climate there is spring all year. Not too cold or hot. I am building my home there and when I retire from dance, I want to return to the home I was born in. I have been around the world but feel that Dali is closest to me. It is the best for me to return there. Behind me is the Cang Mountain and before me the Erhai Lake. The environment is still protected. Dali was once a powerful kingdom. Its culture is like a magnet."

"But some people say Lijiang is Shangri-La," I asked incredulously. "Others say it is somewhere north of there; they say Zhongdian. So you seem to say it is Dali. Where is the road to Shangri-La? Does it begin in Dali?"

She just laughed, then smiled and closed the fan of her outstretched fingers. "People say Yunnan is Shangri-La because its environment is pure and the ethnic diversity is sustained. So Lijiang is also Shangri-La and so is Zhongdian, for that matter. Every place in Yunnan thinks it is Shangri-La. To find it, follow the Tea Caravan Trail. It will lead you from Dali to Lijiang and past the Tiger Leaping Gorge to Zhongdian. Along the way, there are many sacred mountains. They are sacred to each of the peoples who live there."

"Sacred mountains?" I asked, disbelieving. "What makes a mountain sacred?"

"After leaving Dali, you will go to Lijiang. There, the Jade Dragon Mountain is sacred to the Naxi people. Climb the mountain, but it is cold and difficult to stay there. Lijiang's water comes from the melted snow of the Jade Dragon Mountain. The people pray to the mountain. So you could say they drink sacred water, it is the source of life and death. People go to the mountain in search of 'death love'."

"'Death love'? What's that?"

"Young Naxi boys and girls believe in joint suicide to go to an ideal third world. They believe another world is even better."

I was even more confused. Sensing this, Yang Liping continued, her thoughts uninterrupted. "Then go north of Lijiang to the Lugu Lake. The

Mosu people there believe it is Shangri-La. The women choose their lovers but never marry. The Mosu are a bit like Tibetan and Naxi mixed. Their life is very free and it is a matriarchal society. Because women can give birth, thus property should transfer to them. They think they are the useful part of the society; and love is natural there because women set the rules. Their belief is different — they feel that love is the highest state of conscious awareness, so they strive toward it instead of regulating it with laws and rules of marriage."

"So where is Shangri-La then? Lijiang or Lugu?"

"Zhongdian claims to be Shangri-La," Yang Liping smiled at my confusion. "Because the higher altitude makes it a Tibetan region. The natural environment is more protected. The environment is retained best. Due to high altitude, life there is not easy. People are few, so its natural environment is protected. Going further north is the sacred Tibetan mountain, Kawagebo. People going there in late autumn feel there are flowers growing in the snow, and yaks and sheep run free. There is no barrier between people and nature."

"Why?"

"Because they live a life that is close to the mountains. When you live close to the mountains, you can better listen to what they say. They are the words of spirits," she explained.

"So there is a way to communicate with a sacred mountain?" I asked incredulously.

"If you want to hear the words of spirits," Yang Liping said, no longer smiling but with one long outstretched fingernail pointing in an uncertain direction, "Then I suggest you find the mountain."

Loft Dreams

"A fact that will interest you is that Henschell began our collections of Chinese art...He made a remarkable journey... He did not leave the valley again, but it was his ingenuity which devised the complicated system by which the lamasary has ever since been able to obtain anything needed from the outer world."

—*Lost Horizon*

To find the mountain, I first looked for the artist, Ye Yongqing. I remembered that he usually hung out at the Loft, a series of factory warehouses in downtown Kunming. Ye had converted these into artist studios, interactive galleries and coffee shops. I knew if I went after midnight, I would find him somewhere in the gallery, maybe drinking coffee, maybe drinking beer.

Kunming's streets were empty. A light rain had fallen. Shadows of leaves of leafy trees reflected in puddles in the street. The taxi drove through the puddles. It passed a river and crossed through streets with open-air restaurants. At a place where an alley breaks out from the street, but where nothing else is distinctive except the front wall of a factory, I hopped out of the taxi. I remembered that to find Ye

Yongqing's Loft, I had to first look for the place where one would least expect to find an artists' commune.

I faced the flat brick wall of the factory, then stepped into the dark alley and followed it until I heard laughter. The laughter came from Ye Yongqing. He was inside the main gallery sitting on a worn sofa drinking beer with Fang Lijun and Yue Minjiao, two of the most famous artists in China. Known for painting themselves with bald heads and laughing faces, their art fetched the highest prices for Chinese paintings on the market. At Sotheby's Hong Kong, their works auction for millions of Dollars.

I wondered why each of the artists had shaved their heads. It

seemed that shaving one's head like a Buddhist monk had become a counter-culture statement among artists who wanted to be alternative in China.

In the West, artists often wear their hair long. Between the 1980s and 1990s, China's emerging artists copied everything from the West, and wore their hair long too. Now that Chinese art was commercially accepted by mainstream Western collectors, galleries and museums, artists sought independent expression of individual personification. To achieve this, they shaved off all their hair.

I was to learn that this new form of anti-conformism had already come to represent a new conformity. China's independent artist individualism had finally been recognized by Western mainstream art critics, entirely for commercial reasons. In fact, this recognition had already taken the alternative out of the art. It was now all about commercial conformity to Western art tastes and Western perceptions – often distortions -- of what China is today.

I asked Yue Minjiao, "Why do you always paint yourself laughing? Is it some kind of laughing at society, or some kind of social protest through laughter?"

He looked at me as if I was stupid and replied directly, "I paint myself because I like myself."

"You like yourself?"

"In fact, I like myself very much. I think I am wonderful."

I was dumbfounded. Turning to Fang Lijun, (whose paintings fetched over US$ one million), I asked how he felt about the commercialization of Chinese art. His success had already stimulated him to begin making ceramic busts of himself looking like Mao. They were for sale in some Beijing galleries.

Fang Lijun snapped, "Commerce and art are not in conflict. Art and money are always in a relationship." Then looking at me as if I were some idealist, he added crisply, "Art is money. That's all."

I thought about Van Gogh and Miro; about Picasso's own view of art being political when he finished "La Guerre". These artists all fought against conformity, and in the case of Miro and Picasso they were expressing through their abstraction a rebellion against facism, then on rise in Europe. Clearly there was none of the same politics or even emotion in the art being created by these Chinese artists. It was all about money and ego — in a way representing the prevailing mood and values absorbing China today. Maybe as a social commentary, their outlook was reflected in their art. It all reflected China's rise from poverty to wealth, and an all-enfatuating nearly fanatic worship of money that had become a national phenomenon.

It was this national obsession with money and ego that had driven me to leave Beijing. But by coming to Kunming, I had not gotten far away enough from it. Clearly, I would have to go further. I asked Ye Yongqing where to go to find that sacred mountain, which Yang Liping talked so emotionally about.

Ye Yongqing — himself an endless source of knowledge about Yunnan — thought about my question for a while, both eyes looking up at the steel-wrapped wooden beams supporting the factory roof of his loft studio. Ye Yongqing concluded that Yunnan had quite a few mountains. Many of them were sacred. To find them, I would have to trek a route called the Cha Ma Gu Dao — Ancient Tea Caravan Trail.

Ye Yongqing explained that the trail was once only wide enough for

horse caravans. Now it had become a road. The route crossed through Tibet, connecting China with India. This made it the southern parallel equivalent of the Silk Road, which crossed from China to India through Xinjiang during the Tang Dynasty (618-907 AD). For this reason, Ye noted the Tea Caravan Trail is often incorrectly referred to as the "Southern Silk Road". Actually, it was not used for trading silk.

The Silk Road ran from ancient Tang capital Xi'an in Shaanxi Province across the northwest deserts of Gansu and Xinjiang, across passes in the powerful northern Karakaroum Mountain Range to India. From central Asia, distributors sold silk to Europe. Silk, craved as a precious commodity in Europe and the Middle East, was moved west by camel caravan. When the caravans returned, they brought Buddhist scriptures from India to China.

In parallel, the Tea Caravan Trail ran through Yunnan, crossing the Himalayan range of Tibet to India. The trail started from the rich red earth tea growing region of Simao that produced the famous Pu'er tea. The first leg ran from the hot jungle hills of Xishuangbana to the ancient Bai kingdom of Dali, then to the Naxi kingdom of Lijiang. From Lijiang, the trail connected through steep mountain passes to the Lugu Lake, the isolated realm of the Mosu tribe — the "Nation of Women".

Another trail, the main route, continued from Lijiang, passing the Tiger Leaping Gorge, and then on to the sacred White Water Terraces — the source of Naxi Dongba religion — up to the Tibetan regions of Zhongdian with its great Songzanlin Temple. The old cowboy town of Zhongdian was a key outpost on the route. It followed narrow hairpin bend trails through mountains over 4,000 meters above sea level to the Tibetan cowboy town of Deqin near Kawagebo — one of the eight Tibetan sacred mountains.

From Deqin, the trail, only accessible in dry seasons of spring and fall, ran north crossing through the Kham regions of Tibet, eventually arriving in the holy city of Lhasa. From Lhasa, caravans continued to the Panchen Lama's capital Shigatze on to Bhutan, Nepal, Sikkim, and then at last, India. The journey from Dali to Lhasa could easily take four months; to India, a year. Caravans of nimble ponies with bells tied to their harnesses, colorful Tibetan blankets and bright tassels click-clacked and ding-danged their way across this dangerous route.

The economics underlying the caravan trade was straight-forward. The Tibetan plateau, desolate and cold, does not support agriculture. Tibetans, who are nomads by nature, survive by raising sheep and yak. They drink yak butter milk all day and all year long to fight cold and to

resist the elements of high altitude. But pure yak butter milk is thick and difficult to digest. Sharp tasting Pu'er tea provided the second element of survival. Mixed with yak butter milk, Pu' er tea cuts the butter, creating a tasty, digestive tea. Pu'er is also rich in vitamin C. In fact, for many people living on the Tibetan plateau, Pu'er tea became their main source of vitamin C.

Just as silk became the essential fabric to Mediterranean Europe and the Middle East, throughout the Himalayan region people depended on Pu/er tea. Yunnan caravans provided tea, and brought back Buddhist scriptures from Tibet and India. Buddhist philosophy quickly became absorbed into the lifestyles of Yunnan people, in some ways, Buddhism was re-interpreted and localized by Yunnan's varied kingdoms and tribes, each with their distinctive customs and outlook. Just as Yunnan tea became essential to Tibet, Tibetan Buddhism became inseparable from Yunnan.

Through these routes, the northern Silk Road and the southern Tea Caravan Trail, cheap commodities that China produced in surplus flowed West. Spirituality overflowed from India and Tibet moving east along the caravan route to be absorbed by China. In some ways, real globalization of trade and ideas began here.

"In Yunnan, connectivity begins with tea," explained Ye Yongqing. As he rambled on in his stream of consciousness that night about the history of Yunnan's Tea Caravan Trail, imprinting horse hooves in my mind over beer flowing in modern artists' lofts, one thing suddenly became clear. To find sacred mountains, I would have to trek the Tea Caravan Trail.

Beneath the incense fragrance of cigarette smoke clouding at the highest warehouse beams supporting the loft, stories of the Tea Caravan Trail unfolded from the computer bank of Yunnan accumulated knowledge stored in Ye Yongqing's mind. As beer flowed through the evening, the trail unwound before me. Little did I realize, by morning, I would be following it.

DALI

Follow your own query and own thoughts.
It is for you to find your own road.

The ancient kingdom of Dali was a walled city-state. It was really a mini-country onto itself until defeated by Kublai Khan and absorbed into the Mongolian empire in the 13th century.

The walls stand today. Within, narrow streets wind around canals running from the Cang Mountain behind this walled city to Erhai — the 'Ear Lake' — spread before it. Water trickling and babbling through these canals comes from the mountain mist in summer, and snow in winter.

Before the Cang Mountain is the Erhai Lake. They call it the 'ear' because it seems shaped like one. There are different stories about the lake, it is said when Avelokitshavara, the Bodhisattva of Compassion (whom Chinese call 'Guan Yin'), witnessed the suffering of humanity, she shed a tear. Some say the tear became the lake. Many come to the lake to look for the tear.

Alongside the incline where valley and mountain connect, artists have opened art studios, meditation and yoga retreats which intermingle with the bars, cafés and hill tribe craft shops. The community has become a kind of bohemian retreat. It feels a bit like Kathmandu, Ubud or Chiang Mai did in the old days. People are not interested in discussing what is happening in the "real world". For them, it is an illusion. Here, what is happening in Dali is real. They come to Dali to remove themselves from the unnecessary, to create their own reality. Some stay for just a while, others for lifetimes.

The Cang Mountain is covered by snow in winter and mist in summer. The mountain range spreads across the width of the lake and its reflection can be seen within, like a mirror in the early morning when waters are still awaiting sunrise. That is when you can hear the Bai people singing. They push flat boats onto the lake, toss fishnets and awaken the morning with songs.

The Bai dress in bright blue tunics and don blue Chinese army-worker hats. The tunics are said to have come from the traditional dress of the Jiangnan southern Yangtze region, which is the Bai's origin. Probably about five hundred years ago or more, they were pushed west and settled here. The hats came when Mao Zedong's Red Army trekked by during the Long March. Some left their hats. The Bai have been wearing them ever since.

Today Dali is caught between the richness of its past and the crassness of an encroaching commercialism that threatens to change it forever.

Glasshouse on a Lake

"Never had Shangri-la offerd more concentrated loveliness
to his eyes; the valley lay imaged over the edge of the cliff,
and the image was of a deep unrippled pool that matched
the peace of his own thoughts."

—*Lost Horizon*

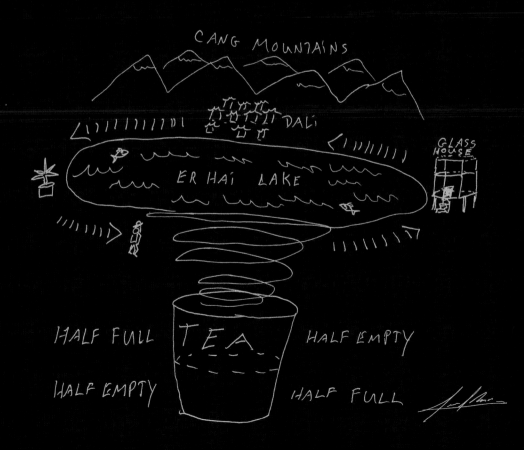

Ye Yongqing traveled with me to Dali
and introduced the artist scene there
to me. He insisted on one artist I had
to meet. His name was Zhao Qing. He was no longer painting pictures.
Instead, he was making glasshouses.

Ye Yongqing led me around to the far side of the Erhai Lake to an
untouched Bai village named Shuangxing. In the village center, Bai life
was encapsulated as women worked and men played mahjong in a two-
story pagoda-style building that was actually a stage and a teahouse
at the same time. I watched a few games of mahjong — broken teeth,
broken days — as the mahjong tiles clicked away, marking the passing of
time.

Blue cotton cloth, babies in quilts bobbing on the back of mothers walking softly through stone streets of age-worn broken stones. The narrow cobbled streets led to courtyard homes, each of which had big cows and little pigs tucked under their houses built on stilts beside the smooth water of the Erhai Lake. lifestyles about to be broken ... I feared it was the last glimpse of a valley on the brink of change.

Blue batik fabric caught light of shadows in courtyards of red pillars supported by blue stone carved as outstanding as any ancient mansion in Beijing. Stone worn thin by centuries of feet. An elderly Bai woman slings a piece of pig's thigh freshly cut onto a nail over the doorway to air and become the sweetest Yunnan ham.

Light blue cotton is everywhere, surrounded by sounds of children laughing in the valley. Women with baskets weighing on their foreheads stoop over, purple velvet vests folding under the weight. Maybe we all carry burdens throughout our lifetimes.

Crumbling alleys of dirt packed walls, tile chips extending from walls and graveyards on the hill from where the dead can see green mountains overlooking the lake. As the sun was setting, the mountains reflected jade in tranquil, turquoise water. I listened to the lake and thought about having a conversation with the mountains.

The sound of mahjong tiles clicked through villages amidst stories of legends in mountains of mist and stone paths leading nowhere. We followed the stone path to where it stopped, at the edge of the lake. Ye Yongqing waved to a fisherman on a flat wooden boat. He came to dock momentarily as we stepped aboard and pushed off to an islet where Zhao Qing was building Yang Liping's glasshouse beside his own.

Imagine a house made of glass built on sharp rocks overlooking a lake. This was Zhao Qing's art. The house and lake were inseparable. High tide pools actually entered the garden, and streams flowed under stone and glass coffee tables. The house, a collection of interlocking rooms — some made of glass with steel frames, others traditional stone and gray brick — created a living piece of interactive art in the form of a home.

Ye Yongqing walked me through the construction site of Yang Liping's home, which was being built by Zhao Qing. The entire lower floor was designed, deliberately, to be entirely submerged by water when the lake is at high tide. Another alcove was designed for Yang Liping to sit overlooking the lake to meditate. This is Zhao Qing's approach to design. It is art.

When I met Zhao Qing, I thought he was a monk. His head was shaven and his appearance was that of a Tibetan lama. He showed me the room he meditates in and the Bodhi tree growing beside his house. An artist, he did not do art. There were no paintings or sculptures. His studio was the space around him and his art the houses he created to interact with that space. This interaction extended to his every movement. Every drop of tea he poured radiated a feeling of deliberate yet unstructured care.

"Lots of people think I am a monk," Zhao Qing spoke with a smile. "They say I look like a lama. Actually I am not. I have my wife and children. I enjoy comfort too. I am not a monk, but I meditate and cultivate myself. This is something everyone should do as part of their lifestyles. It does not necessarily mean you are a monk."

Like Yang Liping, Zhao Qing also came from this village of Shuangxing. I asked about the village and life alongside the lake, living in a glasshouse, and Dali.

"This place feels very rich because the materialistic pressures on life are very little. People here in Dali do not care if you are famous or just an ordinary person because we live close to nature and those things are irrelevant. I will give you an example: a nomad is very strong, this you can see in him. He is healthy as he lives close to nature, and he is happy. So don't forget your health and happiness. Many of us are searching for the things we already have."

I was taken aback. "But don't they want what we have, urban lifestyles and money to spend on consumer goods?"

"We think we are so hardworking, so busy, there are so many things we must do. They may think differently."

"Like how?"

"Many people believe in 'causational effect'. It is related to Buddhist philosophy. Many people here in Dali think about their actions being related to an end result. In my later days, I will have to retrieve the result of my action. So I must consider what I am doing now. It is like going to a bank. You borrow the money, later you must return it. If you give others help or kindness, later they will return it."

"Is that why people are drawn to Dali, not just for the scenery but the way of thinking about life? Is that why Yunnan is becoming a magnet for artists?"

"I feel comfortable here in Yunnan. Many artists come to Dali searching for this. They are looking for an energy that they cannot find in their developed urban environments. They are looking for a lifestyle and a mood of spirit. This is not a material question. The measure of a person is not how many assets he has, how many friends he has collected, nor how many relations he has. For me, returning to Yunnan and my home in Dali is happiness. It is not so complicated."

"But by coming here, the artists are away from their markets. People are leaving material comforts behind, right?"

"Requirements in life are different for different people. Some are very simple. Like, can I live in a place where the air is clean and there are not so many people? If you have enough assets and money, then after you have bought all the things you can afford, maybe you just want to return to something as simple as that."

"Like this glasshouse? It is a piece of art integrated with the lake and peninsula. You must have designed it for meditating?"

"It is not for meditating. It is for my lifestyle. Three years ago, I came here to write a lot of poetry. But now I write less. I meditate more."

"How does poetry evolve into meditation?"

"From another place, take a look at yourself. From an independent state, examine your own existence. From one dream realm, look into another. That is poetry. It is not your expression; it is that other person looking from the outside expressing you. It is a kind of romantic

knowledge of another who can see more clearly than yourself telling you about your situation. Poetry is just the language used to do this. A poem is very close to you, but when you read it, you'll understand that its meaning is deeper and broader than the language written on that piece of paper. It is not just yourself as a person communicating. You have become the source for channeling social emotional trends into the language you write. The mystery of poetry is in this."

"And meditation?"

"The same as poetry."

"So can one reach Shangri-La by meditating, or writing poetry?"

"Shangri-La exists within each person like a tree. It has branches, leaves and roots. It opens a flower. That flower — is it related to the branch, leaves or roots? Maybe it has no relationship at all. It is a hope or an ideal. But it does not necessarily exist, or its existence is very peripheral. But then, how did that flower open?"

"So it exists?"

"It exists in the realm of my family, friends, home and environs. It is a creative moment in each person's life. Like when I see the lake here or watch Yang Liping dance. It is that creative space captured in a moment."

"How can it be found?"

"You should ask yourself. Follow your own query and own thoughts. It is for you to find your own road."

Mountain Dreams

"He saw no reason to inveigh against the prevalent fondness for the tangatse berry, to which were ascribed medicinal properties, but which was chiefley popular because its effects were those of a mild narcotic."

—*Lost Horizon*

A STREET IN DALI

Ye Yongqing traveled with me to the ancient walled kingdom of Dali — first stop on the Tea Caravan Trail. We stayed in a guesthouse owned by a Tibetan named Nyma, who offered foreign backpackers yak butter tea. Actually, it was just Lipton tea with milk and cinnamon. Most did not know the difference and enjoyed drinking what they thought was traditional Tibetan tea. So on the Tea Caravan Trail, Nyma's guesthouse did a booming business in Lipton. Actually in Dali, since the region was still lowland, traditionally there were no Tibetans.

Dali was home to the Bai ethnic minority. The Bai built their houses with bright white walls and gray-tiled sweeping roofs. Their homes looked more like those of the river villages in Jiangsu Province. The Bai even dressed the way old people in older villages of Jiangsu still dress today. Except they wore blue cadre hats, long out of fashion elsewhere

in China. They said these hats were left behind by the Red Army when
they marched past here on their Long March. The Bai liked the hats so
much, they adopted them as part of their traditional dress.

Hundreds of years ago, the Bai migrated from the Yangtze River
basin. They left the basin and moved west, finally settling in Dali. In
some ways, as migrant descendents of the Yangtze River, they are pure
holders of China's past. As ethnic minorities, maybe because of their
past isolation, they have been able to preserve aspects of Chinese
culture that the Han in China have already forsaken.

"But look at what's been forsaken," Ye Yongqing pointed to the newly
built gray brick walls around Dali. "In the past, these were made of dirt
and stone. This is Yunnan. But the government tore down the original
walls, used gray bricks to create something that looks like a replica of
the Great Wall around Dali. This is not part of Bai ethnic culture. It is
something from China's north, stuck here in the far southwest. Maybe
it's Manchurian?"

Ye Yongqing explained that the Cang Mountain is sacred to the Bai
minority living beside the Erhai Lake. The Bai are Buddhist. The lake
is said to have been left there when the Bodhisattva, Guan Yin, shed a

tear upon witnessing the suffering of humanity. So the lake is a tear. It reflects the mountains like a mirror. The mood of the mountain, like a soul, changes with the seasons. In summer, the mountains are covered with mist; in winter, snow.

We walked through the gate. Night markets were unfolding around us — newly made antiques, ethnic minority silver bangles and belts for sale — giving Dali's alleyways a feeling more like Chiang Mai than a city in China. Wandering through the alleys, we walked up a street lined with bars and cafés. It was named "Foreigner's Street". Actually, there were hardly any foreigners there; mostly Chinese. Artists from Beijing and Kunming had re-congregated in the bars. Many had studios in Dali — places to paint, away from the pressure of cities like Beijing. In Dali, there was no pressure.

"If anyone says he is doing business in Dali, he is just joking," Ye Yongqing whispered. "Here, everybody is really just unemployed. Doing business in Dali is just an excuse to hang out."

Tourists passed. They passed by on the street outside, passing in all directions. They did not come into the shop because it did not sell those things that tourists would want to buy. So we wandered up the street to see what they were buying. We found a shop run by a Hong Kong guy who had a very un-Hong Kong beard. He rode a motorcycle and sold silver in his shop, the kind of silver bracelets and earrings that might seem cool if you spent a lot of time riding a motorcycle. Before coming to Dali, he had lived in Chiang Mai.

I suddenly felt the similarities between Chiang Mai and Dali — the lazy bars, kick-back coffee shops, tribal trekking, and of course, shops like this selling little assorted handicrafts. I asked about the silver crafts he sold. What sold the most — earrings or bracelets? He showed me a tiny silver box. It was so tiny that hardly anything of substance other than powder or puff could be put into the box. I suddenly realized that he was making his money selling powder and puff, not silver handicrafts.

We went upstairs. The stairs were steep. They were broken, narrow wooden steps that twisted through rafters untouched except for time. It was easier to fall down than to climb the steps. On the second floor, the room was tiny and crowded. It was crowded because it was so tiny. Actually, there were only a couple of people there. A Chinese girl was strumming a guitar; a foreign boy sat next to her smoking a fragrant pipe. It smelled like perfumed fragrance rolling off the tip of an incense stick in a Hindu temple that somebody had placed there in reverence before dreaming of lotus flowers awakening before dawn. Clearly, they were dreaming of lotus flowers. Our presence awakened them. It was not yet dawn.

Walking down the narrow steps, we stumbled back on the street and wound the bend in an alley, crossing stone slabs crisscrossing creeks running between stone gullies. Rounding the corner, we glimpsed a pale yellow light that shone lemon in the dark with the words: "Bird's Nest

Bar". I suspected this is where birds descend. Behind a steel high security door, there was a very low security bar. We entered into a haze of sweet smoke. The birds seemed high, but here we could descend.

"People here are like birds," explained Ye Yongqing. "They migrate with the season."

We left and returned to the street, then passed a small shop. It smelled of sweat incense. The incense came from India. Ye Yongqing pointed out that lots of gypsies hung out on the sidewalk, sometimes even on the floor inside this shop. In another time and place, they would have been honored as hippies. But that was a bygone era. Now, in Dali, they are just gypsies.

He pointed to a small pretty gypsy with long hair. She wore a thin tank top. Her hips were wrapped tightly in a long batik skirt hanging to her toes. If one did not look twice, one might suspect she was Balinese. Stepping up from the sidewalk into her shop, Ye Yongqing introduced me. Her name was He Xin.

He Xin giggled half a giggle and then smiled, unsure of who I was or why I had come. A long-haired foreigner squatting beside her quickly tucked away his pipe in the cloth wrapper, which he placed in a bag slung on his shoulder. The transaction had already been completed. So he just walked away. He walked quickly and remembered not to look back.

He Xin giggled. "This is my boyfriend." She nodded to a young man lying on the floor stirring a pot of coffee, pouring it into little finger sized cups, which he drank half through his lips and half through his nostrils. He handed me a cup. I suspected there was more in the brew than just Yunnan coffee beans.

He Xin's boyfriend came from Taipei. He was fed up with the noise, pace and hectic frenetic bustle of Taipei. So he went looking for a misty

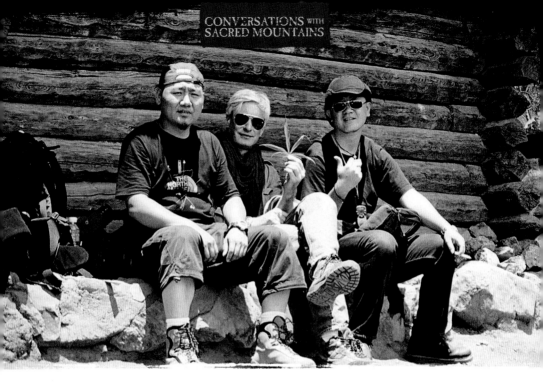

place south of the clouds. He went looking for a place close to mountains and lakes. He was looking without looking when he met He Xin in Chengdu, Sichuan's capital, one of China's rock-and-roll capitals, a place of rain and clouds. They decided to leave the rain. So they traveled south of the clouds and came to Yunnan.

He Xin had a friend who had opened a bar in Zhongdian. So they decided to go to Zhongdian. They wanted to find their friend and sit in his bar, maybe on a barstool, maybe on the floor. It did not matter, as long as they were in Zhongdian. That was their single objective as they left Kunming, following Yunnan's ancient Tea Caravan Trail to Zhongdian. The first stop on the trail was Dali. They never left Dali.

They found a place to live on the side of the Cang Mountain — a timber house on stilts. They raised dogs and grew grass. They slept with the dogs. They smoked and sold the grass. Together, a big family — warm when the mountain is wet with rain — they listened to the rain and dreamed of mist on the lake.

He Xin said her dogs were healthy on the mountainside and this was from the freshness of living on a mountainside. Her boyfriend pointed to the dog sleeping beside him on the floor. "If our dogs weren't healthy, they would not sleep like this," he explained. I looked at the dog. The dog looked stoned.

He Xin explained she was becoming a professional tattoo artist. I asked her what art she had tattooed so far. Looking sideways both ways, she seductively pulled up the corner of her long batik skirt. She hinted I could look at something underneath. She wiggled her five toes and I could see a large marijuana leaf design imprinted on her ankle. I asked her what else she had tattooed. She just pointed at the leaf, and

smiled. I asked her again. She continued to smile.

She smiled with that unsure smile that spoke of misty dreams drifting among clouds in the Cang Mountain. Even though we sat in her shop, I could tell she was still somewhere else, maybe lost in the mountains. We talked about rain on the lake amidst the smell of Indian incense. I could tell she was dreaming. So I asked about her dreams.

"He Xin, what's your greatest dream in life?"

"To go to Zhongdian," she answered. "I want to go there to find my friend."

"And what will you do when you find your friend?"

"Sit in his bar."

"If it's your greatest dream, then why don't you just go there?"

"After arriving in Dali, we cannot go. We just can't get the energy to move to anywhere."

"So you will stay here forever?"

"Here there are mountains and lakes. But we won't stay here forever. You cannot stay anywhere forever, so we cannot stay here forever. But for how long we will stay, who can say? So we just stay."

"Stay, for what?"

She just shrugged her shoulders, giggled, and said she was waiting. I watched her eyes. They were listening to the sound of incense burning.

I asked, "What are you waiting for?"

"I am waiting for the mist to pass."

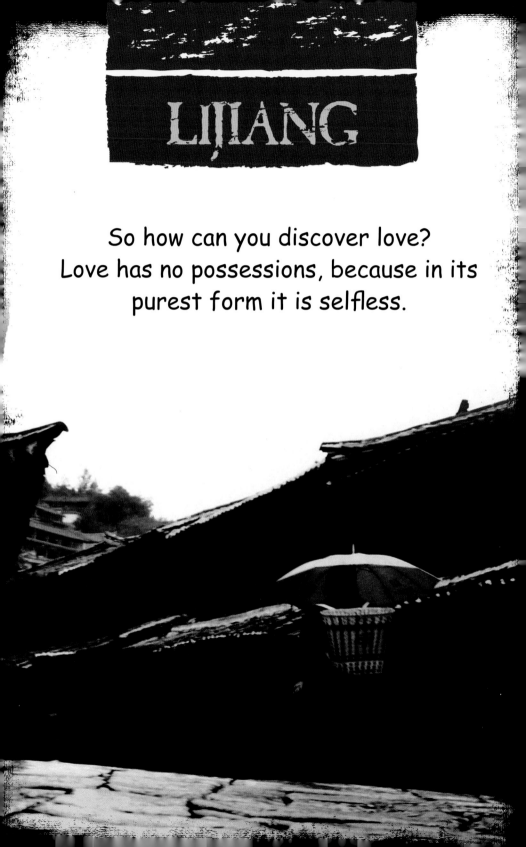

LIJIANG

So how can you discover love?
Love has no possessions, because in its
purest form it is selfless.

Lijiang was the ancient kingdom of the Naxi people. It is a maze of narrow streets interconnecting around interlinked canals. The buildings are made of gray brick with bright red wooden pillars supporting curving tiled roofs. The streets are full of energy as Naxi people call to each other from the windows or chat along the canal. The main market, Sifang Street, is a wide opening in the narrow maze where people gather for daily business or conversation and it is always full. At night, children light candles on paper lotus — releasing them into the canal where they float away with just a wish.

The altitude here rises 2,400 meters above sea level and one begins to feel that one is leaving the warm south and heading toward the Tibetan plateau. In ancient times, Lijiang was the border; the last outpost of the Chinese empire at the edge. Beyond were mountains and nomadic lands of the Tibetan people who often came to Lijiang to trade furs for supplies.

The Naxi possess the oldest form of written language still in use, based upon hieroglyphic drawings, which look a lot like modern art. Their religion is Dongba. It merges Buddhism from Tibet with ancient

wizardry, and the Dongba priests or wizards serve as intermediaries between the dead and the living.

In the "between" is a floating "Third World", which is neither heaven nor hell but something better than ordinary life. It is a place where forlorn lovers sometimes choose to go — committing suicide to avoid separation or to perpetuate their love. Suicide was a fundamental aspect of Naxi traditional life. Almost every Naxi family has had some history of love suicide. So the Naxi understood how important death is to life, and living.

The place for committing suicide is their sacred Jade Dragon Mountain. It is, covered with snow all year and its face is covered by mist in summer. Upon the upper reaches of the Jade Dragon Mountain, one can find an ancient alpine forest. A clearing in the forest offers the best view of the mountain's peak. That is why so many lovers chose this spot for suicide. The air is fresh and cool. Its mists echo the sadness of those who have come here to leave. Its drifting snow carries moisture. The snow awakens flowers in spring.

Searching for Joseph Rock

"Search is too strong a word...you can't search a country half as big as Europe for one man. All I can say is I have visited places where I was prepared to come across him or to get news of him...There were traces of him up-country for a little way, and in my own opinion is that he probably made for the tribal districts on the Chinese border."

—*Lost Horizon*

In 1933, James Hilton wrote the book Lost Horizon in which he described Shangri-La as a mystical land in the Valley of the Blue Moon, beneath a snow-capped mountain. Here, people whose life centered about a Tibetan monastery enjoyed freedom of love and lived for hundreds of years. Fantastical, Shangri-La became a generic term for some state of bliss or harmony. In the 1960s and 1970s, hippies looking for corners of the planet where drug taking was not tightly regulated ventured into Nepal, which seemed to have the characteristics of Shangri-La. Others thought the place Hilton described might be in Kashmir.

The great irony is: James Hilton never visited the Himalayas, or Asia, for that matter. So one might presume that Hilton's story was entirely contrived. On the other hand, the strange thing about

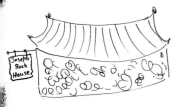

Hilton's book, amidst the fantasy he created, was his precise description of certain locations, landscape features and cultural traditions, which could be attributed to northwestern Yunnan, specifically the region through which the Tea Caravan Trail ran. The Tea Caravan Trail was arguably at its height of use when Hilton wrote this book. In recent years, it has come to be known in the tourist industry as the "Shangri-La Trail".

This all began when different counties in the region began arguing over which area was the "real" Shangri-La. Neighboring parts of Sichuan and Qinghai provinces, even Tibet Autonomous Region argued over the Shangri-La name. Pricking up its ears on hearing the jingle of tourist cash,

all of western China, it seemed at one point, joined the debate, which became a full fledged competition for an approval from China's central government as to which location would be permitted to bear the official title "Shangri-La".

The debate became most acute in Yunnan where Dali, Lijiang and Diqing competed fiercely for the title. Eventually, the title was given to Diqing Prefecture, which contains the two counties of Zhongdian, with its Songzanlin Temple, and Deqin, the location of Mount Kawagebo, both described almost specifically in Lost Horizon. Amidst the moaning and groaning of other would-be Shangri-La regions, the central goveroment gave its tacit nod to using Shangri-La as a means of promoting tourism in all of the southwestern region of China and the Tibet Autonomous Region, thereby broadening income horizons on the "Lost Horizon".

It does appear that locations described in Hilton's book matched these places — actually the region as a whole. Hilton wrote about a World War II plane crashing in the Himalayas. Wrecks from the Chenault's Flying Tigers can still be found near Lijiang. The free-love society described by Hilton could pinpoint Lugu Lake. The "lamasery" he described appears to be Songzanlin Temple in Zhongdian and the pyramid shaped snow-capped mountain fits Kawagebo. But where did Hilton get this information?

Amidst the dispute, I was curious about where Hilton got his ideas. It was said he had researched the region in the British Library. But what was he researching? Tibetan texts? It seemed too improbable. The book was clearly written by somebody with only distant knowledge of Asia, mostly guessing about the culture. So I began to do research in the guesses.

Indicators pointed to another source, an Austrian-born American named Joseph Rock, a contemporary of James Hilton. Rock, a botanist

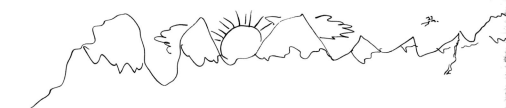

who spent time in Hawaii, settled in a village outside of Lijiang, where he stayed for seventeen years as representative of the National Geographic Society. From here, he traveled extensively, sometimes staying in a fortress he built on an island in the Lugu Lake, home to the Mosu "nation of women", to Zhongdian and Deqin. He provided regular reports on the geography and customs of the region, accompanied by extensive photographs, to National Geographic, which published them over this period. James Hilton was most likely reading the reports and looking at the pictures, drawing upon the various cultures of separate locations explored by Rock, merging these together into his colorful novel, describing everything at once in a single rotation.

By following the book Lost Horizon from Dali to Lijiang, I searched for clues. In Lijiang, I asked local Naxi people, who pointed the way to a village made of red rock walls and timber rooftops nestled in the shadow of the Jade Dragon Mountain. Why Rock might settle here became apparent when mists enveloped the mountain. As I climbed the steep trail leading to this village, Naxi women in blue tunics smiled without teeth, and pointed the way further. I knew the direction must be right, because apparently Rock was the only foreigner who had ever lived in this village.

I found the home of Joseph Rock. He had lived in a simple Naxi timber and red clay house with a tiny courtyard, in the shadow of the Jade Dragon Mountain. Some of the older villagers still remembered him. One remembered, as a young boy, how his father had worked as a carpenter for Rock, making benches and fixing saddles. Now an old man, his eye was infected and as he spoke, liquid drained from the corner down through the aged cracks in his cheek, like a river rushing through a valley, dripping precariously on his Naxi blue tunic. I wondered whether he could see all right. He spoke as if he saw Rock's shadow before him. I asked him if he remembered Rock leaving the village. He remembered that day quite clearly, could see it as if it was yesterday. Did he miss Rock? He waited. They all waited for Rock to return. He never did. In some ways, it seemed they had been waiting their entire lives for his return. In some ways, maybe they are still waiting.

Another old woman remembered her parents working for Rock as bodyguards. In those days, bandits hung around in the mountains. So when Rock went on botany expeditions, Naxi guards had to follow with

guns lest robbers rob him of his plants. I wondered what they would do with the plants in a place covered with trees anyway. Fear of robbery was so serious in those days, when Rock stayed north of Lijiang at the Lugu Lake, he had to build a small castle on an island upon the lake. Fear of robbers was that real.

What kept Rock here in this village? Did he have a girlfriend? No. In fact, according to all the old villagers I spoke with, throughout Rock's seventeen years in this village, nobody remembered him having any female companion at all. Though one Naxi later told me that Rock had a Mosu girlfriend at the Lugu Lake, where he built a castle on an island. A few years ago, the child, a mixed Mosu and Caucasian, had been spotted in villages alongside the lake. But nobody knew anything else.

So I wondered what Rock was doing here in this village at the foot of the Jade Dragon Mountain and whether botany was really so interesting after all. I could not imagine. So after talking with the old folks who remembered his shadow, I crawled up the broken wooden staircase, a half ladder, and entered Rock's room.

This was where he wrote and slept. There was nothing in the room except a brazier fire like those used by Tibetans in this region to keep warm at night, his writing desk, and a bed. The writing desk had nothing on it. So I sat in his chair and wrote. While writing, I noticed the black coals in a fire long gone. With a simple bed and table with only a Tibetan rug underneath, Rock's life must have been spartan, lonely, and completely devoid of anything except the space between his own silence and that of the mountain. So I sat there in his wood and clay house and stared at silence. I remained fixated in the emptiness between us and the mountain. For a moment, I was beginning to understand Rock, and maybe how one begins to have a conversation with a mountain.

Finding Xuan Ke

"And he knew, too, that his mind dwelt in a world of its own, Shangri-la in a microcosm, and that this world also was in peril."

—*Lost Horizon*

In the old city of Lijiang, with its graceful arching rooftops and narrow canal connected alleyways, one can find a theater where every evening an old generation, which has seen too much come and go for one lifetime, sits down together in a moment that seems a sigh of collective harmony, and plays a tone of ancient music. It might have actually been the music of Han Dynasty China, now forgotten by the Han Chinese people themselves, but remembered and preserved by the Naxi.

The man responsible for preserving and reviving this tradition is an old music teacher, who himself witnessed more than one might ask for or want in a single life. Resigned but sardonic, he smiles under large glasses and hosts the evening of Dongba music and Naxi culture. He is there every evening, never misses a night, and is the very fabric of this tradition — kept alive in the Dongba orchestra he has brought together. "It is sad," he explains to the audience, "as over the years many musicians on this stage disappear and leave us." Meanwhile, younger musicians sit beside the old masters and hopefully, the tradition will continue.

After the performance, I sought out Xuan Ke backstage. I was curious and asked him, "You have been the most active individual preserving Naxi culture. But now, with an onslaught of Westernization, do you feel its traditional values are endangered?"

"Because Lijiang is now open to tourism," he said with a sigh, "it brings both good and bad. For instance, Westerners come here; they are only interested in culture. They come with one purpose, asking 'where are the traditions, where are the people still living in their own culture?' They are not interested in going to disco or fancy restaurants. So they end up coming to my concert hall. Here, they can listen to the original music played by Naxi people. Of course, it is for tourism, but it sustains the culture. The musicians are old, and it gives them employment and purpose."

"Maybe this is a last window to Naxi culture?"

"The Naxi culture is disappearing," he said with a nod that did not signal resignation.

"Is it because of the onslaught of Western tourism, or the Han?"

"This is one thing. We know from both China and Lijiang's historic records that before the 14th century, the Naxi people received little Han culture. Then in the 14th century, there were two important

years and dates: August 1381 and February 1382. These periods were very important because the Ming Emperor Zhu Yuanzhang banished 350,000 Han people and soldiers here; to these remote places, because they had different ideas from the emperor. At that time, Lijiang was the center of the Naxi nation, which had a population of 47,000. Suddenly, 350,000 Han people and soldiers arrived. When people come, culture comes with them. So everything changed. For instance, marriage customs, poetry, painting, even festivals. So many Naxi traditions were lost."

"More specifically," I asked, "how did the influence of Han culture water-down or change Naxi traditions?"

"Let's talk about weddings, for example," Xuan Ke shrugged, "in the traditional Naxi dictionary, there was never a word for father or wedding. Children did not know who their fathers were. It was a matriarchal society and free love was a very important part of the culture."

"So is that where the idea of suicide love in Naxi tradition came from?" I wondered out loud.

"The Dongba priests believed love was a paradise between Heaven and Hell. They believed that Hell only burned below and Heaven opened above. God was kind. And people who entered Heaven would be welcomed by their past ancestors. So many lovers killed themselves by eating poison or jumping off the cliff into the water. They felt this was safe. Better they go to that paradise in between."

"They ate poison?"

"They ate a black herb, which is very special — it enters the throat and immediately it closes it and nobody knows why you die," Xuan Ke whispered as if revealing a secret. "It is immediate. So if lovers did not want others to know the history of their deaths — the romantic reasons kept secret — they took this herb and closed their throats. Lijiang can be called the suicide capital of the world. Almost every family in Lijiang has, in its history, love suicide."

"In Western thinking, this is tragic," I implored.

"In Naxi thinking, it is romantic," he insisted. "They can go to another world between the material world and Heaven. It is a floating world. Then their parents who survive the suicide lovers will undertake ceremonies once or twice a year with Dongba priests chanting to celebrate the happiness their children enjoy in this third floating world, and eventually the previous generation of ancestors will open the gate of Heaven and they can enter the upper paradise, which is different from the floating world between."

"Despite the onslaught of modernization, fundamental Naxi thinking was not changed?" I asked. "This differs so much from the current atmosphere of abject materialism. These days, people will not die for love, only for money."

"This is a key philosophical difference," explained Xuan Ke. "What is the world for, the dead or dying? Death is not dying. Death is not dead. It can mean or be explained like this — dying is not the end of the life or beginning of the new life. It is a place between death and life."

"This is very difficult for many new to Naxi culture," I exclaimed.

"Often, marriage was decided by the parents, not by the young people. They often decided to marry off the children before they were

born. The parents never thought about their children's future, only their own."

"This must have been an external cultural influence upon the Naxi," I commented. "In the Han materialist tradition, marriage, as an institution, is for merging assets. So the concept of giving up accumulated material assets for an abstract ideal such as love must have been almost heretical. The idea of dying for it, unthinkable."

Xuan Ke explained that under such circumstances, "The Dongba priests would then tell stories like the priests in churches of Europe did. They would draw a picture of paradise in the minds of these youths, a place easy to go to. A place without any dirt, power struggles, money struggles, no theft. There are always wine, songs and women. Anything you like is there."

"So is this where the idea of Shangri-La came from?"

"No." Xuan Ke shook his head again. "Shangri-La is not the real natural world. After Hilton published his book Lost Horizon, people believed it is a good place or better than the war years we lived through. So people think that Shangri-La is paradise, things are much better there. So the new reality is to rush there."

"In your generation, are there still people who believed in this floating 'third world'?"

"When I was young, they believed. When I was fourteen, I went to Kunming and came to know what happened there in the 1930s to 1940s. After that, I was working in Kunming and after 1957, put in prison for twenty-one years. After that in 1978, when I was released, I searched for my girlfriend and asked to return to Lijiang, where I became a teacher of music. At that time, things had already changed a lot. Free love like Han Chinese boys and girls enjoyed could be seen everywhere. But in the countryside, we still heard news of some cases using black poison. Some lovers even used TNT — they would tie themselves together and smoke a cigarette to blow themselves up, even in the middle of the highway. So when I came back in the late 1970s, and even in the 1980s, there were these stories, lots of stories. We could still hear this kind of story. Then they became fewer."

"This is a very ancient Naxi tradition, but at the same time a very modern idea," I pried.

"Why?" Xuan Ke seemed surprised.

"Because young people throw away their material world to die for love or an ideal, trying to pursue a dream and make it come true even if they die with the dream. It is a very romantic and even modern ideal."

"I think it is better to escape," he exclaimed. "Many people hate war, their children to be sent first to Korea, then Vietnam, now other battles. And their children never come back. How can they find the dead bodies? So these people hate war. They are angry. Better to keep away from battle and war. How can it be a good society? How could they stay longer? Some people have the power concentrated in their hands so they decide war or peace. Just a few big people decide this. It is unfair. So people want to find a place like Shangri-La. If it is true, they will sell their cars and houses — the whole package — to find that dream world of Shangri-La. So for the feeling of modern people, this is not only in China."

"Is the 'third world' then another truth?"

"If it is true," sighed Xuan Ke, "then it will happen. If not true, it is a dream. Keep it in a dream; it is very wonderful. If we find a real Shangri-La and paradise, it is a waste of time. But if this is in a dream, then this dream is better than the real stories."

"Do the young people believe in the dream anymore?"

"No, they have given up."

"Without the dream of the 'third world', will their hopes be lost?"

"They will be lost."

"Is it a tragedy?"

Xuan Ke thought for a moment pensively. He then answered with a forlorn look in his eyes. "When a people lose their culture and beliefs, it is a crime. We name ourselves Naxi. If the Naxi lose their tradition and culture, and dream of what they dreamed before, then everything will be lost. Then there will be no Naxi again in the forest of human beings. If you lose your dream and culture — your blood vessels — then this tree will fall."

"How do you look at the contradiction between tourism, which keeps the culture alive and which also kills the culture? You saved the Dongba music and bring it to the tourists, to the outside world. But tourism also destroys culture. How do you deal with the contradiction? "

"It is not what will happen, it has already happened."

"So tourism both saves and destroys culture?"

"Westerners want to save culture and help to save culture of others, even give a helping hand. People are starting to get a better education, but how can they help when they only have one idea for their society? There is only one idea and way of saying things. So how can they get better education? I received my education before the 1940s. I think in some parts, the old education system is better than nowadays, in those days, we had free choice and if we wanted to study music, we could."

"Is Lijiang a stop on the ancient Tea Caravan Trail?"

"Before, in Tibet, the main food was yak butter tea with lots of oil and fat. Without oil and butter, it is a cold place, so you have to take a dose of yak butter every day. But precious Pu'er tea cuts the fat, providing vitamins. They do not grow tea in Tibet. So Sikkim, Nepal, Bhutan, Darjeeling all came to depend on tea. From there, the tea caravans brought back goods from India and with them scriptures and

Buddhism. This was the tea area of Yunnan the Tea Caravan Trail went from Simao and Pu'er, through Dali and Lijiang, to Deqin, Changdu, Lhasa, across to Sikkim and Darjeeling. In the old days, it took four months one way. Yes, you are following the Tea Caravan Trail."

"Is it the road to Shangri-La? "

"That is a difficult question. I made Zhongdian Shangri-La. That was my effort. On December 28, 1998, I was the first one to speak this idea to the journalists. Then BBC, NHK all came to interview me. I always changed my mind but it was too late, because it was already fried, delicious and served to the eaters. I was in Kunming before 1946 and remembered such a place that combined Tibetan, Naxi and Han culture. My mother and grandmother were born near there, so I wanted to share with people some good things. Before I said it, it became true and became the official name. Then after I said this, they stopped cutting wood in the ancient forests there. So it is better than before. There was no other name for Zhongdian and nobody there knew what Shangri-La was. After I told the journalists Shangri-La was in Zhongdian, everyone there began making money from tourism and stopped cutting trees. In the end, it is better for the trees."

No Dreams

"She continued, with a bright smile that seemed more an attachment to her face than an illumination of it: 'You see, I've been thinking over the way things happened to bring us all here, and there's only one conclusion I can come to. There's a mysterioius power working behind the scenes. Don't you think so, Mr. Conway?'"

—*Lost Horizon*

Near Lijiang is the village of Su He. It is just a village, a very small one. In Lijiang, people call Su He "Little Lijiang". They say if you want to get a last glimpse of "old Lijiang", you have to go to Su He.

Because of these comments, tourists who feel Lijiang is too crowded with other tourists will go to Su He. Soon, Su He will be crowded with those fleeing tourists. Then it will become stuffed with Lonely Planet style guest houses and banana pancake cafés. Like everyone else fleeing the Lijiang crowds, I went to see Su He before it stopped being a tiny forgotten village and turned into a suburb of Lijiang.

Su He consists of one street that ends when crossed by another, like the letter "T". Entering the village from the bottom of the T, I crossed a meandering stone bridge, water babbling beneath. Su He's entire existence probably once depended on this river. Now, it depended on tourists.

Older women, with kindle wood on their backs, stooped over as they walked. Some spent their entire lives like this, carrying kindle wood; so do we, but never realize it. We think it is something else. Really, it is just kindle wood. I thought about this, following them down the cobbled streets, with a backpack slung over my shoulder, filled mostly with unnecessary things. Sometimes we spend our entire lives carrying burdens on our backs and carry them into the next.

The backpack was heavy, so I stopped for a rest. An old, red wooden panel caught my eyes. It depicted Buddhist motifs of Buddha, a deer, and some other animals. I figured such a quaint carved panel must be from Su He. I asked the shop girl, a pretty young Naxi. She shook her head. Was it from Lijiang? She shook her head again.

"No," she replied sharply with indifference. "It's from Suzhou."

"What? You are bringing wooden antique panels from Suzhou, near Shanghai, to Su He to sell to tourists who probably just came from

Shanghai. What about your own antique panels? What happened to them?"

"They've all been sold out a long time ago. We have to give tourists local antiques, so we import them from other provinces."

"So Shanghai tourists go to Su He only to buy what they could have bought in Shanghai?" I was beginning to feel the weight of my own baggage. I rested for a while. Pressing my backpack against the wall beneath her shop window, I sat on the stone steps of the shop by the door, leaned back and took a deep breath. The young Naxi shopkeeper sat down next to me. "Anything else you want to buy?"

"Not really. Actually, I just want to talk to you for a while."

"What do you want to talk about? If our shop does not have it, I have friends running other antique shops in our village. I am sure we can find it for you, whatever it is you really want."

"Actually, I do not want anything. I just want to ask, have you ever heard about the 'Third World'?"

"Third World, of course, it is a Naxi tradition. In ancient times, young boys and girls would commit suicide for love. That way, they went to the Third World. They believed it was a better place to be, suspended between life and death. There, love could last forever."

"So you have heard of it?"

"Of course, I'm a Naxi."

"I know, but do you believe in it?"

"Believe in what, dying for love?"

"Yes, so you can go to the Third World and experience it forever."

"Love is not worth dying for," she replied matter-of-factly, shaking her head. "I believe in reality. That sort of thing is simply not realistic in our world anymore."

An older lady dressed in traditional Naxi blue who was sitting on the stone steps had overheard our whole conversation. She snapped sharply at the girl in disagreement. "The Third World is romantic," she expounded. "Imagine two people deciding to die together for love, for the purpose of maintaining love forever as can only be done in the Third World."

The young shop girl just laughed back with a shrug. "It is impossible these days."

The older lady hounded the young girl. "It is really sad that our new generation has lost interest."

"Interest in love?" the young shop girl quipped back.

"No," said the older lady in a lowering voice, "interest in believing."

"I don't have time to believe," snapped the shop girl. "We have to be more pragmatic. Love is just pragmatism. We have to make money. If the one you are with is not able or willing to pull his or her weight and make money too, then who can think of dying together? Better to live alone or find someone else."

Last Dreams

"The moon was riding high in a waveless ocean. It came to him that a dream had dissolved, like all too lovely things, at the first touch of reality; that the whole world's future, weighed in the balance against youth and love, would be light as air."

—*Lost Horizon*

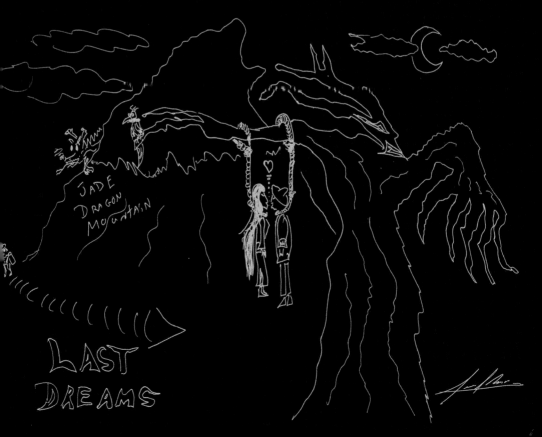

The Jade Dragon Mountain is the protector spirit of the Naxi people. The Naxi watch its changing face, sometimes hidden behind clouds, sometimes white reflecting brightness of the sun. Its melting glaciers provide life-sustaining water.

They listen to its lyrics babbling through the labyrinthine canals of Lijiang, which connect every household with each other. The Naxi people drink and bathe in its sacred water. A new-born Naxi child is washed in this source. So from birth, the Naxi are connected to each other and their protector — the Jade Dragon Mountain.

Many young Naxi couples have chosen to commit love suicide at the Jade Dragon Mountain. They look for a high point where ancient pines meet the glacial line. Here it is cold, but the air is always fresh.

Early morning awakens with horse bells on grassland before sunrise, echo linkling among surrounding ancient pines. Under shadow of glaciers, a grass plane extends and spreads between forests. Close to the glacial line lies an ancient pine forest. The forest opens before a field always full of yellow flowers. For some reason, trees cannot grow in this field. The forest line stops abruptly in a vast circle surrounding it without explanation. Some say because so many lovers committed suicide on this spot, the forest stops here in reverence.

Horses graze on grass and yellow flowers, oblivious to what happened here. Behind flower dotted grasslands, sharp white peaks of the Jade Dragon Mountain pierce the blue sky. The feeling persists that this field exists in the presence of a shadow extending from the peak, where glaciers retreat among clouds and horizons cease to exist.

Climbing to this point at sunrise to watch clouds retreat, I heard a single flute crying like a hurt eagle in the distance. Following the flute, I found her sitting on a rock, her long black hair woven into tiny braids hidden under a thick fur hat. She could have been an illusion, except the wail of her flute was real. She ignored my presence and continued playing her flute. Pausing for a moment, she began chanting to the mountain, her voice rising as if it was her intention to shatter the blue sky and pick up the broken pieces afterwards.

"The clouds pray to sunrise that awakens," she whispered momentarily, placing the wooden flute on her lap. "Every day is the first day of time. The mountain rises from crying mists and an illusion of the reality we believed was a previous night appears to only be a segment of imagination long forgotten by the wind. I am sure you understand what I am talking about, don't you?"

Without waiting for my answer, she explained with a sigh, "The rattle of horse bells is elegant upon the mind, especially this early in the morning. It makes one wish to arrive here, to this very place, chanting to the mountain. I come here everyday to play my flute and chant. I do this before sunrise burns the clouds. This was where we hung ourselves over fifty years ago."

I observed the point where a white snow peak pierces the sky. Against such clarity, mists returned and the Jade Dragon Mountain became veiled in a gray that was neither clouds nor mist. Like a curtain, it enclosed spirits who reasoned in silence. They could not be heard because their conversation was the language of snow drifting against blue sun and yellow sky, intemperate in their interchangeability. It was the resounding echo of blue, so clearly heard among tall ancient pines, soaked in mist.

Where horses grazed amidst tinkling bells, in the mistaken words of silence, she beckoned me to sit beneath a tree where many lovers had hung themselves staring at the white peaks of the Jade Dragon Mountain, revealing itself from momentary mists. She asked me to imagine how they felt — ropes around their necks, jumping from an outstretched branch — self strangling while dreaming of mists clinging to the mountain, beckoning life forever in a world of half death, where purity clings to the empty white of snow. It was a place she called the "third realm".

She explained, "According to Naxi tradition, at the Jade Dragon Mountain, there are three realms we can be in. These realms exist simultaneously in rhythm. Whichever one you find yourself in, it is a function of your karma. In short, you determine it."

"Then what are the three realms?" I queried.

"In the first realm that the ancient Naxi scriptures describe, 'Flies and mosquitoes are the masters of this world. Its roads are full of poisonous snakes. Ants the size of one's shoes are everywhere.'"

"That does not sound like a place we want to be in," I remarked under my breath, which suddenly felt cold as wind slid off the glacier above. "What does the second realm look like?"

She seemed a bit impatient, somewhat irritated as if these things should be understood without being said. "According to the ancient Naxi scriptures, in the second world, there is only winter, no spring, no flowers and no fruits. The summer is very hot, but after the summer, there is no harvest because there is no autumn."

Her breathy voice sounded exhausted. Clearly the thought of entering this world frustrated her inner senses. She felt repulsed. I did not know whether I should ask anymore. I realized we had crossed a line. But because my question remained unanswered, I had to ask it.

"So those are the first and second realms. They don't sound like nice places to be. Maybe our world is really like that too. Instead of flies and mosquitoes we have traffic and telephone marketing. But didn't you say there are three realms? Sorry, but I think you forgot to tell me about the third one. What happens if we enter it?"

She immediately perked up, no longer slouched over in a seeming state of depression. She gently shook her long hair back from her face, two large silver loop tribal earrings caught some strands of hair. The sun reflected from a glacier above. Her eyes widened obtusely. "According to the ancient Naxi scriptures, it is said that only in the third realm can you find a world where there are no mosquitoes or flies," her voice rose with excitement. "There, you can ride on the backs of tigers. Horses and deer work to plow the fields. Wild roosters serve as

clocks. Trees give yak butter and provide freshly steamed bread. There is no hunger nor pain nor worry in this world. Meat is eaten instead of rice and milk is drunk like water. There is no sadness there."

"It sounds like Shangri-La."

"It is the realm where lovers go when they commit suicide together. There, they can make love twenty-four hours a day, three hundred and sixty-five days a year, and the years pass on forever. Can you imagine such a place?"

"They really will commit suicide to go there?"

"They feel their souls will go to the third realm, a land of eternal bliss."

"So that's why they choose to commit suicide?"

"It is not that they choose; it is their wish."

"You mean because their families won't let them marry, they commit suicide as a form of protest; something like Romeo and Juliet, right?"

"Not always. Actually, there are many situations when a couple might just want to die together to keep their love. When you get older, life changes, we change. But young love is a very pure feeling. Many do not want it to change so they commit suicide together. That way, springtime can be eternal."

Her words settled in my mind like dusts of white snow drifting from the peaks above us. I thought about Palestinian youth committing suicide for a cause and ideal, maybe driven by the emotion that they have nothing else to look forward to in life, and hopes taken away from them. But to commit suicide to keep alive something such as love — not even an ideal, just an emotion or at best a feeling of hope — was altogether something else. Or was it? I asked her to explain more.

"Actually, it is not unusual for a middle-aged couple, married, with grown-up kids, to come here and commit suicide. They do not want to grow old; to see themselves and their love fade. So to keep it alive and perpetuated, they commit suicide. It is their choice. They prefer to live in the 'third realm'. Maybe it is better to die believing in something like this than retire and wait to die not believing in anything at all."

Together, we sat on a rock under an ancient tree, where lovers hung themselves. She pointed to the old cedar branches where ropes were once tied and asked me to close my eyes for a moment and imagine a couple embracing as their necks stretched and cracked under the siege of a long rope, too short to allow their feet to touch the earth.

Trees clung to ridges. Mist clung to trees. A meadow spread before us. It was full of flowers moistened by scattering snow moved when the glaciers shift. "Imagine a world of free love, where people die to perpetuate a memory while it lasts, before age or disease forces us to stain and lose it?" she asked. "In such a world, one reaches a state of the non-material. Here, we realize that possessions are not worth holding on to. Nothing lasts. Only complete detachment brings happiness."

"For most people, this is really hard to accept," I reasoned with her. "It seems like such a waste for a young couple to lose everything — their whole lives before them — just for a silly romantic notion, a passing emotion, like love."

"You simply do not understand," she sighed with faint exasperation. "Most people live their lives without ever really experiencing the feeling of love. That's why we Naxi people value it so much. It is more important than life. So we die to perpetuate its memory."

"But is it really worth dying for? I think anyone — Westerners or Chinese — will not accept this idea."

 She shook her head. Exasperation had stretched. It was bordering on frustration. But I could feel her

 patience cool down as a breeze passed by us both, carrying broken yellow flowers floating in circles before scattering in purposeless directions.

In a soft but deliberate voice that rose above a whisper but fell short of spoken words, she explained everything all over again for the last time.

"By making love before death and holding on to the feeling, one finds a place between two states of mind. In one, you are leaving, and the other, arriving. This feeling cannot be perpetuated in life. You do not want to leave life because you are attached to its possessions. So how can you discover love? Love  has no possessions, because in its purest form it is selfless. If you cannot reach that understanding, then love is just an illusion, because you are only trading and leveraging it like a commodity for some kind of possession, maybe material, maybe egotistical. As long as you cling to these things — possessions and ego — then you cannot find love, because it can only be found in a perfect state of emptiness and detachment. At that point, you have nothing."

"So that is why young Naxi lovers commit suicide after making love?"

She looked at me quizzically with the black core of her Bodhisattva eyes, as if tempting me to die, and asked with a breath of glacial mist, "Can you imagine how the sound of love tastes when the clouds depart?"

LUGU

I like Mosu women...
They just do it and when they finish,
they do not ask for anybody's approval.

After climbing narrow passes through the land of the Yi tribes, one arrives at the Lugu Lake coming over the crest of a mountain. The lake spreads like a vast mirror exuding calm upon its waters.

The Lugu Lake is home to the Mosu "nation of women", arguably the last matriarchal society left in this world. They adopted many Tibetan customs and practice Tibetan Buddhism.

Their sacred mountain is Ge Mu. It is a female spirit that rises beside the lake, reflecting their values and social hierarchy. The lake is their mother, the mountain their protector spirit. The Mosu people love their lake and mountain.

In olden days, men plied the Tea Caravan Trail and women stayed behind. That is how they came to rule their society. While many customs are considered ancient, much of their thinking is quite modern. Actually, it would be considered avant-garde, cutting edge in most Western societies, where a medieval morality still rules. Maybe the Mosu are more advanced in thinking than most in China, where Western consumerism and materialism are equated with being modern. There is actually a difference.

This difference became clear when crossing a mountain pass and seeing the lake spread before me. It was just so calm — a sheet of perfectly clear water, a mirror on the moon and sky. I looked into the mirror and asked myself, "What makes the Mosu different?"

Because the Mosu are on the edge between Naxi and Tibetan areas, their culture reflects a mixture of Dongba and Tibetan beliefs and practices. So if there is something we can learn from the Mosu, it is how we can live on the edge.

Tiger Folk

"At all other times the horizon lifted like a curtain; time expanded and space contracted, and the name Blue Moon took on a symbolic meaning, as if the future, so delicately plausible, were of a kind that might happen once in a blue moon only."

—*Lost Horizon*

If I went north, it would take me to the Lugu Lake. I would have to travel over mountains. In my mind, I would have to join the caravans.

Had our II pruning hence caravans up mountain passes through pines and mist — you are entering the clouds. Mists arouse stones fall, roads collapse. Log cabins amidst green moss covered forests, mud-red rivers run. Mists flow into valleys. Rivers cascade into mist.

There are rivers. They run fast and deep and cannot be crossed, but only followed. Even in the old days, when horses following the Tea Caravan Trail came to these rivers, they had to be strapped to rope pulleys and suspended across the rivers.

Following the rivers is not so easy either. They twist through valleys that become canyons where rocks fall and destroy roads you might want to follow. But to follow the roads, you must follow the rivers. Avalanches are frequent. Rocks collapse regularly, especially in the rainy

season. They fall on the roads and block your way. So remember to walk around the rocks.

When avalanches occur, wait at a teahouse along the river and watch it flow past. Frustration at passages being blocked and time lost dissipates into a calm awakening that maybe this is a nice place to sit beside the river and let one's ideas about time flow past as well. Sometimes, you can wait in a teahouse along the river all day for somebody to come along and fix the road. Sometimes, you have to wait several days.

Maybe nobody wants to fix the road. Maybe nobody is here to fix it. Or nobody thinks that anybody else wants to follow it, so they simply do not bother to move the rocks. Even after they move the rocks, the road may no longer exist. It has already washed away. The rain did it.

Rain in the late summer of Yunnan has a way of doing that. It can do

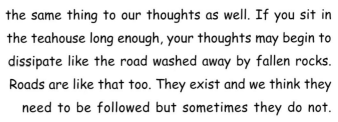

the same thing to our thoughts as well. If you sit in the teahouse long enough, your thoughts may begin to dissipate like the road washed away by fallen rocks. Roads are like that too. They exist and we think they need to be followed but sometimes they do not. So when rain comes, we may see our road dissipate into the river, and feel a great sense of loss. It takes so long to get here and that road is written so clearly on the map and even described with precise detail in the guidebook. But if you arrive there and find it totally washed out, the feeling can be one of total loss and frustration.

That is where the teahouse comes in. It is a place to sit and wait for the road to be fixed or maybe to decide to backtrack and take another route not described in the guidebook. Maybe an Yi tribesman will come pick you up and take you up a footpath never written in the maps because the mapmakers never knew it existed.

This is the fundamental importance of teahouses. They give shelter, and are places to wait and allow thoughts to disintegrate and new ones to arise. They are stops on the way following roads that do not lead in the direction intended and may lead in the one meant to be followed. Sometimes, we need a total collapse of the road we have been following to realize it was not the one we meant to go down.

So maybe you will just have to wait several days at the teahouse by the washed out road running beside the river. You can always take your backpack and throw it into the river. You can toss it off the roadside and watch it tumble through brush and hang precariously from a tree that might have stood in its way. Think twice. Maybe you will climb down the side of precipice and retrieve your backpack. The river is not that

close anyways. Its passing is only an illusion. Maybe you never needed the things packed on your back to begin with.

When it is time to move on, stop drinking tea and continue your journey. This time, follow the river. The mists have not parted, so you must follow the river. The river is more reliable than the road because it has been here longer. It has cut into the valley to form a canyon, wearing away ages with its presence. There are green mountains on both sides of the river that cannot be climbed, because the river has cut so deep that the mountains forget they are separated by water.

The illusion that a river can be crossed gives one the sense of terror that he will be stranded on a bank, churning in rough water for an eternity even if it is only a vague recollection of a grain of sand in time, which has elapsed within the inner most recesses of one's memory. It is a moment from another lifetime repossessed in a feeling of need. Its recollection signals the beginning of finding a way.

As you lose yourself in the valley of the Gold Sand River, which becomes the mighty Yangtze, you become acutely aware that water cuts through rock. You are entering into earth. Now you will rise with the altitude and reach clouds that have evaporated into mist. They are dissolving before your memory and finding their closest comfort in the moisture, clinging to moss hinged to crippled trees in mountains above the valley. Moisture will seduce their senses like pungent wine weighing temperature down into forming concurrent matter in patches of sky until clouds become rain rushing into rivers. The rivers pour across gorges, moving rocks across roads in their ways until they find a source in the great river below, before they eventually evaporate into mist.

Rivers run deep, they churn. A single viewpoint may be dangerous. White tops of golden and brown are grains of sand churning in the river. Grass above the stones are wet and sharp, you may cut yourself or slide into the valley gripping with both hands a rock as cold and smooth as a snake's skin. Hold on to the snake's tail as it slithers away. Realize that clutching a rock is a momentary pleasure undisturbed by fear of the river rushing below. Do not fear the sound of the river as it calls to you. Like time, it is passing by and if you stay here long enough, you will grow old like the mountains and be forgotten by the passing of time.

As the mountains rise, the trail follows. The river becomes a thin snake winding below. At certain points, it can barely be seen because the mountains feel so high. For a moment, it is easy to be deluded that

we are flying like eagles. They know the truth. We are only ascending
the mountains and still far from the sky. In villages along the trail,
there are mountain folk. They carry burdens on their back as well.

Firewood tied in bundles, crops picked in the late afternoon from
the mountainside — they are carried by Yi women walking in long lines
along the trail, their black headwear stretched like great bat wings on
each side of their head. They sometimes smoke long thin pipes and are
not too worried where the trail leads, as they know it will eventually
take them either up or down the mountain.

So who are the Yi? It is really hard to say. They are not one tribe
but so many sub-ethnic groups divided by the mountain on which they

live. Because it is hard to say that Yi are really the Yi, it was easier for anthropologists to call them that than to write more dissertations about it.

The Yi differ from other tribes of northeast Yunnan. They slash and burn for a living, growing crops until the soil is spent and then move somewhere else. So their villages, built on the sides of mountains, are always temporary. They are semi-nomadic, semi-sedentary.

The Bai of Dali became known for their business acumen — trading tea on the Tea Caravan Trail. The Naxi of Lijiang are famed for their Dongba sorcerers who are intermediaries with ghosts. Mosu to the north were legendary for their powerful women and matriarchal world. The Yi tribes, however, were feared for their notorious stealing. They survived on the side of mountains and learned to steal from the caravans passing below. They plundered because it was just so easy.

The Yi pray to fire and tigers. Each Yi woman wears a laohu — tiger bracelet — and a bochun around her neck. The bochun is a metal coil that looks like two thirds of a solid ring. I wondered if it was worn to protect against tiger claws aimed at the neck in the old days when tigers roamed the mountains, or just an ornament to keep one's neck straight?

Above their tiger bracelets, both arms are tattooed to the elbow. Strange tattoos — they are only green dots in disorderly lines like stars sparkling across the summer Yunnan sky. The green color comes from mountain grass, so Yi girls wear the mountain on their arms

throughout their life.

All Yi girls have these dots tattooed on their arms. They are symbols of their people. They are one with the mountain, practicing slash and burn culture, moving from place to place. Their houses are temporary because every few years, their village moves. In fact, they have no assets other than their bracelets and tattoos.

Nation of Women

"It had not occurred to him to picture women at Shangri-la; one did not associate their presence with the general practice of monasticism. Still, he reflected, it might not be a disagreeable innovation; indeed, a female harpsichordist might be an asset to any community that permitted itself to be (in Chang's words) 'moderately heretical'."

—*Lost Horizon*

I first heard of the Mosu people and the Lugu Lake from Yangerche Namu. She left Lugu — the Mother Lake — as a teenager, wandered to Shanghai, then to Beijing, where she sought an audience with the Tenth Panchen Lama. Throwing herself at his feet, she begged for help. The Panchen Lama arranged her entry into the National Minorities University. After graduating, she became a performer, author and then celebrity.

The Mosu "nation of women" is arguably the world's last true matriarchal society. At the Lugu Lake, women rule. The women choose their lovers, but never have husbands. Children never know their fathers and do not care. Property is held by women, not men, and passed from mother to daughter.

"Zouhun" ("walking marriage") is the tradition where a Mosu girl chooses or changes her lover. Mosu homes have a "flower chamber" built near the entrance of their courtyard houses that is separated from the main compound. A young girl will signal interest to a potential lover by touching the palm of his hand with her fingertips. Then she will stay in

the flower chamber that night. Her lover can visit her after dark and leave before sunrise through a "backdoor", which every Mosu home has for this purpose.

The "walking marriage" concept has been expounded and exploited by Chinese media, who see it as a sexual fantasy that fits the current atmosphere and urban values of absolutist materialism. In the touristy side of the Lugu Lake where hotels are located, Sichuan prostitutes have set up shop dressed in Mosu costumes. In turn, Yangerche Namu became a sort of "sexual celebrity" in China because other than writing about her childhood at the Lugu Lake, she wrote about her foreign boyfriends as well.

Yangerche Namu has written several books in Chinese, which focus on her foreign relationships and play to this Chinese fantasy concerning herself and the general stereotype about the Mosu. She has written one book

in English, which is a very moving story about her people and culture
and serves as one of the best anthropological explications about this
matriarchal society, probably since Joseph Rock.

The concept of "walking marriage" makes sense in a modern context.
While the Han build a lot of cement and glass thinking they are modern,
actually their thinking process is mostly quite feudal. While the Mosu
live in log cabins on mountainsides by the Lugu Lake, their thinking in
contrast is quite modern.

Think about it for a moment. People get married and they divorce,
the lawyer bills and expenses hurt, fighting affects the children, maybe
throughout their whole lives. The Mosu had this figured out long before
we did. They do not need to pay lawyer bills or alimony, because in a
"walking marriage", when the current of emotion changes, everybody is
free to just walk away.

It all began with the Tea Caravan Trail. Mosu men worked the
caravans. Because the route to Lhasa took months, a round trip to
India might end up taking years. The route was hazardous — subject
to rockslides and snowstorms, and the Mosu women never knew when,
or if, their men would return. So the women tended hearth and farmed
the land. Logically, property passed through maternal lineage. It all
made perfect sense. In modern society, seven out of ten marriages end
in divorce within the first five years. While we are stuck paying lawyer
bills wondering what happened, the Mosu had everything figured out a
long time ago. Ironically, thanks to Yangerche Namu's books, the world
now knows about it.

Yangerche Namu's home is a large traditional Mosu two-tiered
courtyard, which doubles as a guesthouse. It is far from the tourist
village, built alongside the Sichuan border of the Lugu Lake, with
the Mosu's sacred mountain shadowing behind. To reach her home, I

123

drove my jeep along narrow winding roads, many sections of which had collapsed under wet season rockslides in summer.

There is a dock stretching into the lake outside the front entrance to her home. Within, in the back section, is a large earthen hearth. Her mother still tends it. Beside the hearth room is Yangerche Namu's own room, the entire wall of which is covered with silk that has dozens of small Buddha prints upon it.

"In Han culture, the dragon is on top and phoenix on the bottom," Yangerche Namu explained, pushing long black hair aside with her fingernail. "In Mosu society, the phoenix is on top and the dragon on the bottom."

"Does this symbolize the role of women in Mosu society as being dominant?"

"I like Mosu women," she laughed instead of answering. "They have a good sense of humor, are good in bed, kind-hearted and hardworking. They are like the wind when they work. They are strong in the face of problems. They never leave the problem to the last day and are never sad. In the village, you can see the Mosu women working, smoking cigarettes, taking care of babies, carrying stone and wood. They have no fear. They just do it and when they finish, they do not ask for anybody's approval."

"You were born here, but now live in Beijing most of the time," I asked. "Where do you prefer to be?"

"This is my home — clear, healthy, warm, together. The whole society should be like this family of mine — warm and happy together."

"Why isn't society that way?"

"It has forgotten that women are the nucleus of society."

"Women?" I asked.

"The women!" she said forcefully, making a fist.

"So is this the last matriarchal society?"

"Our tradition is strong but under some threats," she sighed, then laughed again. "When the door opens to the tourists and everybody comes, there will be some problems in keeping our traditions, though maybe not that much. Because even when more Mosu leave home and come out just like me, they will find that some things at home are good and better than elsewhere. We have peace and love in our lives."

"When you left the Lugu Lake, you traveled all over the world. You wrote books about your international boyfriends and became famous."

"Maybe I had a lot of boyfriends, but I am not that famous."

"Certainly you became a celebrity."

"I became a celebrity because I am creative, intelligent and work hard, not because of my boyfriends."

"Did international jet-setting change your values?"

"After going around the world, I must tell you, I would rather stay at my hometown than going anywhere else. Now I want to come back to support schools and do things for my community. I have built a museum to retain Mosu culture here at Lugu. It was a lot of money for me to build this, but I want to return something to my people."

"Are you able to cope with outside impact entering through the door of tourism?"

"I never liked people telling me how to do things, so I won't tell Mosu how to do things. I built a guesthouse to show my people how to make a homestay more comfortable to the outsiders, and in a way, this protects our culture at the same time. For instance, we have the flower chamber and hearth room, but we also added modern bathrooms for visitors."

"What struck you the most during your visits to the United States?"

"There are many similarities between the American Indians and my people. So when I was in Santa Fe and Taos, I found their culture so warm. Actually our values, relationship between humanity and the environment are similar."

"I have been following the Tea Caravan Trail," I explained. "In each section, there are sacred mountains. For the Bai people, it is the Cang Mountain beside the Erhai Lake. In Lijiang, the Jade Dragon Mountain is sacred to the Naxi. Here at the Lugu Lake, do the Mosu have a sacred mountain as well? "

"For us Mosu, we have a Female Spirit Mountain. It stands behind my house and looks like a huge lion. In fact, the Han Chinese call it 'Lion Mountain'. But we Mosu call it 'Ge Mu'. Inside the mountain, there is a big cave, with lots of natural stone formations. It is a huge cave. When Mosu women have trouble giving birth, they go to that cave. The first time I went there, my Mom's best friend took her daughter, along with many different foods, candles and incense. Her daughter was dressed beautifully and it was very secretive. At first, I did not know why they went there, that it was because she had trouble having a baby. It was

amazing for me to enter the cave. You cannot just imagine how nature can give so much to this world. Nature is our source. That is why I understand how the Mosu people have so much love for this mountain."

Not far from Yangerche Namu's home is another source. The Mosu call it "Dazi". It is the spring water, the very source of water that flows into the Lugu Lake. For Mosu people, it is the most sacred place along the lake. The Mosu people come here every 25th of July on the lunar calendar. They will take a boat to the site and pray to the source of the lake. When they are finished, they will walk in pilgrimage, clockwise around the lake.

Legend says a boy discovered the place when herding a cow. Actually, they recalled, he discovered a huge fish caught in the rocks and when he pulled out the fish, water flowed freely. Water followed the fish, pouring from the rock. The lake was thus formed.

The origin of this natural spring is marked by a manidui of piled stones and prayer flags leading to the source. Waters are calm. A dog barks, a bird chirps, and a rooster awakens the nearby village. Sun rises on the lake. The smell of wood burning is the awakening of a lake after dark. Water warmed by the sun becomes hot by afternoon. A canoe, dug out of a log, rows across the lake before sunset, which streams in a long narrow line of light across flickers of wave in a lake about to be calmed by darkness.

Yangerche Namu pointed to the source. Then pointed to the mountain. She then told the story of the mountain.

Ge Mu is the Mosu people's sacred mountain. It rises beside the

Mother Lake. The mountain is possessed by a female spirit named Ge Mu. She was once a pretty Mosu girl, who grew up beside the lake, working the land together with other Mosu women. One day, they were tilling the land beside the Lugu Lake when Heaven knew about Ge Mu and wanted her. Rumors spread through villages that Heaven may have fallen in love with her beauty. But nobody could prove the rumors. One day, through a cloudburst, Heaven descended to earth, sweeping Ge Mu into the sky. As she flew under the arms of Heaven's gusts, she cried to her people below. The villages gathered around the lake and cried back, seeing Ge Mu flying between the clouds.

They screamed, calling her back and disrupted the force of Heaven's wind that was carrying Ge Mu aloft. She fell tumbling from the sky back to her people, and small dots along the crest of lake started clustering like ants along the edge of an orange peel. As she fell headlong toward earth, her body disintegrated and re-formed, becoming the sacred mountain. Yangerche Namu had described along the Sichuan side of the Lugu Lake.

Meanwhile, Ge Mu's soul was captured in stillness by another gust of wind. She found herself transformed into a spirit, riding a white horse on a white cloud, floating like an eagle through sky of cobalt blue, and playing a flute that calls a lonely whisper.

The Lugu Lake is pure water suspended above the mountains. It is an oasis of blue, and is a point of connectivity between sky and earth. Ge Mu flies into the sky and plays her flute. She is the protector of peace of the Mosu people.

Yangerche Namu recalled among moments in life she enjoys the most, those sitting beside the lake late at night, meditating on the stars that cling to the darkness above. It is the best time to listen. Sometimes, you can hear the flute.

The Horse Can Tell

"A moment later, chilled and shivering, they were all aware that this was so. With no sound in their ears save the fierce gusts of wind and their own crunching footsteps, they felt themselves at the mercy of something dour and savagely melancholy – a mood in which both earth and air were saturated. The moon looked to have disappeared behind the clouds, and starlight illumined a tremendous emptiness heaving with wind."

—*Lost Horizon*

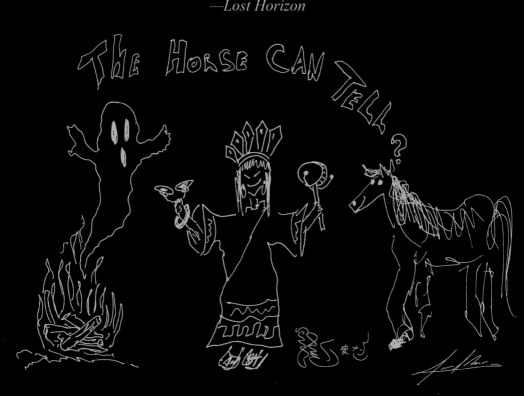

Yangerche Namu's brother was waiting for me on the crest of a mountain where the road turned abruptly above the Lugu Lake. It was a curve marking the end of the road. From this point on, there was only a thin dirt path.

Her brother brought me to the village. There was a funeral. It was for the Party Secretary of the village. I thought of the irony of visiting the Lugu Lake, one of the most enticingly romantic places in the world, only to attend a funeral. But I went along and attended it.

We entered a long cabin, which was the home of the dead cadre. He had been buried underground for days in a section of the cabin used for storage, and also for burying dead people to keep their bodies intact during a period of time set by the Buddhist monks for the funeral. They calculated days carefully on their prayer beads. Their accuracy is never mistaken; the days were followed exactly.

A cartoon-like picture of the dead man had been drawn with crayons on a piece of paper. A paper Tibetan prayer wheel, with a candle burning

beneath it, turned. It rotated naturally, pushed by rising air from the candle. Relatives and friends, basically everyone in the village, came that day to offer food, oil and wine to the deceased.

Flies flew everywhere. They descended momentarily, crawled all over the food for the funeral feast, and then flew away again. Hearth smoke crawled up blackened support poles to mingle with light filtering in from the openings in the roof above.

People from the village cried and howled before the crayon picture. An old man wearing a skin and fur vest, with old-fashioned glasses round as the bottom of a coke bottle, stood in the room announcing to the dead cadre the name of each relative who had come to see him and what they had brought. If a relative brought 10 yuan, the old man would announce they had brought 100. If they brought 100, he would announce 1,000. It gave the impression that currency appreciates in the land of the dead; those alive are cheating on the dead.

The relatives cried and howled; some screamed. Many older people who were close to the deceased seemed really beside themselves. Many of them were accompanied by younger girls, who pulled them away, saying to the dead cadre, "Please rest, we will be well." I was told in the past that

some older people had cried themselves to death. "Why
did you leave us?" they screamed. "Why did you go?" But
after leaving the room, many went about their business.
Some smiled, even laughed. Life just went on as usual.

There were only 120 people in the village, and all were
relatives one way or another. There were only five last names
among all the families present at the funeral. So everyone in
the village was related to one another.

This village near Yangerche Namu's home was very unique, in that
the people were Naxi in origin, not Mosu. Long before anybody could
remember, their ancestors came from Lijiang to Lugu with the tea
caravan and settled. They soon adopted the ways of the Mosu and
lived by the lake. They kept some of the Naxi ways as well. All of this
could be clearly seen during the funeral presided over by Naxi Dongba
priests, accompanied by Tibetan Buddhist monks. In one room, the Naxi
Dongba beat old oiled drums and sang blowing conch horns. In a separate

tent pitched beside the room, a dozen monks chanted.

One stream of blue purple light penetrated from the sky through a hole in the ceiling, where smoke escaped to touch the blue. The light touched the head of the Dongba priest who smoked cigarettes between cymbals. Cigarette smoke mingled with the hearth in enchanting light. It almost seemed as if he could communicate with the spiritual world through the cigarette smoke.

Three horses were then brought before the house. The Dongba priests sang for the horses. Two Dongba priests were dressed as generals to scare away the evil spirits. An elder whispered that the Dongba priests are able to communicate with the dead. They did it through beating a drum and singing prayers that only the dead could hear.

The three closest children of the dead cadre were brought forward and told to ride the three horses to the place where they would burn the body. Whichever horse reached the place first would be significant because the child riding would be the one this deceased person liked the most. Children could live a whole life and never know who was the favorite of their father until he was dead. Only the horse can tell you.

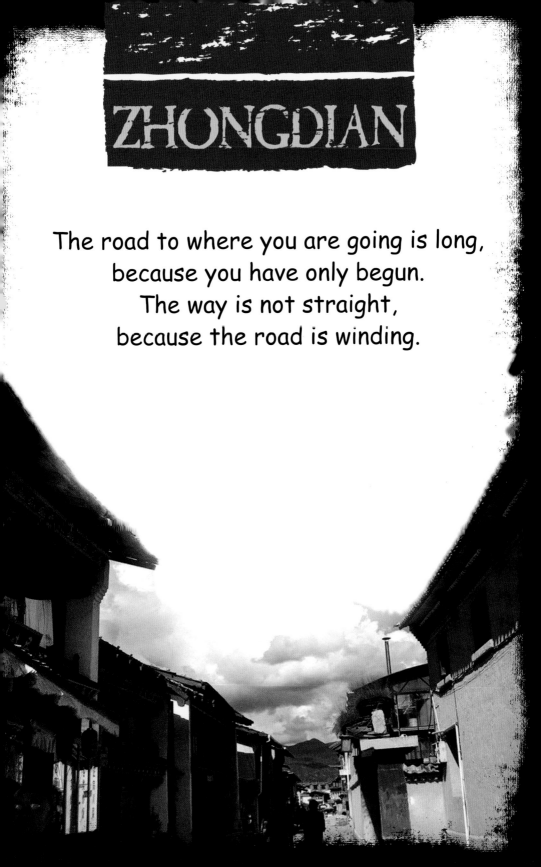

ZHONGDIAN

The road to where you are going is long,
because you have only begun.
The way is not straight,
because the road is winding.

Shangri-La is often described as a grassland filled with yaks and sheep, surrounded by snow-capped mountains and temples with golden pavilion rooftops touching a pure blue sky. No wonder many say Zhongdian is Shangri-La.

The Songzanlin Temple sits in such a valley on a hillside slope between grasslands and sky. On moonlit nights, the chanting of monks can be heard echoing between the surrounding mountains, and the singing of Tibetans fills every village, distinguished by racks made of pine upon which barley is dried. In spring, the valleys are a sea of wildflowers. In summer, horses graze beside rivers appearing from melting glaciers. In autumn, the mountains are golden, in winter, they are wrapped in a soft snow.

It is very possible that much of the content reported in National Geographic by Joseph Rock during the first part of the 20th century was based on Zhongdian. French missionaries entered the valley maybe a hundred years before and built a church that fused French and Tibetan cultures. Today, there are ethnic Tibetan Catholics who go to church in Zhongdian every Sunday. The Songzanlin Temple fits exactly the description of the monastery in the Valley of the Blue Moon of

Shangri-La, the holistic realm described in John Hilton's novel Lost Horizon. North of Zhongdian is Kawagebo, the sacred Tibetan mountain with a face like a perfect symmetrical pyramid, which also fits Hilton's description of Shangri-La.

But among Tibetans, Zhongdian is remembered as a trading stop along the Tea Caravan Trail. Old Zhongdian feels like an old cowboy town of wooden houses — some propped on stilts, others built upon stones along several intersecting streets between a Chinese Taoist temple and a Tibetan monastery. One can feel the mule trains clip-clapping along the stone-laid streets and dirt-trodder paths. Zhongdian buzzes with an old cowboy town trail, leading somewhere beyond the next mountain.

When dust blows down the narrow streets of old Zhongdian, one can sense the emotions of an era when ponies clip-clapped on their way from one place to another without being certain where they were really going. Then, it was a time when across the Himalayas, Buddhism and tea were the connecting forces.

White Water Terraces

"The whole cultivated area stretched for perhaps a dozen miles, varying in width from one to five and though narrow, it had the luck to take sunlight at the hottest part of the day. The atmosphere indeed, was pleasantly warm even out of the sun, though the little rivulets that watered the soil were ice-cold form the snows."

—*Lost Horizon*

Leaving Lijiang, the road wound past the Tiger Leaping Gorge, where waters rush too fast for any tiger to cross. I was told later that such a name was given to this place by the Han people, not Naxi, and it refers to two jutting rocks in the river — allegedly where tigers might cross. Who else could think that a tiger would even try to cross such a perilous ravine as this? At least one can assume that the tiger might be smarter than most people visiting and believing the story.

Water passed like white backs of dolphins or killer whales. The violence of this churning, clearly dangerous water somehow exuded an overwhelming feeling as if one might want to sit on a rock beside the river, or within it, and meditate on a stone.

The narrow, winding road follows alongside the river. Less seen by visitors, away from the hordes of tourists are smaller Tiger Leaping Gorge along the way, tucked in narrower valleys accessible only from a roadside teahouse or homestay.

The land rises past Naxi villages tucked in valleys alongside rivers. The calm of a crowing rooster at dawn and of flocks returning by sunset warms these valleys. The winding road rises and earth transforms from red clay to steadfast pines and ancient cedars. One becomes aware of air becoming cooler, as altitude rises and breath thins.

For a moment, I felt like I was back in my own country, another century ago, walking through America before it happened. Log cabins appeared alongside the road. Pony caravans still passed. Outposts alongside the road offered tea and a place to sleep. It felt as if I was returning to a place I had been to in another lifetime.

Patches of earth slashed and burnt by Yi farmers spoke of villages calling from centuries ago. I was reminded that the government had embarked on a massive program of re-forestation under former premier Zhu Rongji's policy to encourage people to re-plant trees and save

mountains from erosion.

Upon entering Diqing Prefecture, now called Shangri-La County, past the Naxi sacred Haba Mountain, terraces of water in pools looking almost like Balinese rice fields fall into view. At the White Water Terraces, the terraces unfold on top of each other like ice frozen upon a waterfall. Pools of colors form within the terraces — jade, turquoise, deep, penetrating green. Water drips across each terrace upon the next, and the next, fanning out as the terrace unfolds across the face of a mountain reaching from within the pine forests and dropping to grasslands below.

Actually, the White Water Terraces smells like a swimming pool. The terraces are probably formed from natural chlorine in the water. The water flows from sources in the surrounding mountains.

For Naxi people, the White Water Terraces is the most sacred of places. Here, their first ancestor, Dingbashiluo, a grand priest,

  practiced the secret arts of "water falling upon terraces" and founded the Dongba religion. In the misty realm between Buddhism and mysticism, he cultivated the arts of Dongba religion. In the physically abstract realm of the White Water Terraces, he established his center of mystic art. From here, every Dongba priest would have to follow thereafter and the White Water Terraces became the central vortex of his magic power. Dongba religion fused Buddhism, animism and magic. Disciples arrived and left. They brought Dongba magic down from the plateau to the rich valleys of Lijiang, where it took root as both the religion, and cultural core of the Naxi people.

Eventually, the disciples left the White Water Terraces, leaving it locked in mountains. But the Naxi never forgot the source of their religion. Even today, the Naxi would say, "Those who have not gone on a pilgrimage to the White Water Terraces cannot be deemed true Dongba Buddhists." So I stopped at the White Water Terraces on pilgrimage.

Upon scaling the terraces, one first arrives at a hole in the rock the size of a fist. It is said to be a Guan Yin cave. A Dongba priest is at the cave. Before going any further, he will ask you to place your head before the hole in reverence, and burn incense. He will then give you a handful of sacred rice, to be tossed into the hole, and bless you with peace on the road ahead.

Here, I met a Naxi girl named He Xueyan. "My English name is Helen," she explained. "I speak both English and Japanese." Helen was dressed in traditional Naxi attire. The languages were self-taught. Her ambition was to go either to America or Japan. "I learned both languages," she confessed with pride. "If I cannot go to New York, then Tokyo will be just fine as well."

She offered to lead me to a shrine on a stretch of flat field above the White Water Terraces. But before drinking the sacred water of the Naxi Dongba, she suggested burning incense and asked the

Dongba priest tending this shrine to recite in ancient Dongba script. As he unfolded the crackling old papers, characters appeared as living hieroglyphics — illustrations of images almost childlike in their innocence. Symbols of our past, they served as signs of the future.

As the old man ran his long-nailed thumb over the characters, he read as if in a trance, "The road to where you are going is long, because you have only begun. The way is not straight, because the road is winding. The waters flow down because the glaciers are melting. If they melt, there will be no water. If there is no water, there can be no peace. Peace cannot be found through avoidance of conflict, but only by pursuing the truth. If it is not pursued, it cannot be found."

"Now it is time to drink the water," Helen suggested. The shrine was beside an ancient tree that marked two sources of water. One was the chlorine-smelling turquoise that formed the White Water Terraces; the other was pure clear water that one could see in its clarity the reflection of his eyes. This was the sacred water to be drunk. She pointed to the ancient tree dividing the sources. "It marks the point of confluence," she suggested. "But remember, these are two sources that do not intersect."

A Street on the Tea Caravan Trail

"It's a weird place, a sort of world's end market town, deuced difficult to get at, where the Chinese coolies from Yunnan transfer their loads of tea to the Tibetans. You can read about it in my new book when it comes out. Europeans don't often get as far. I found the people quite civil and courteous, but there was absolutely no record of Conway's party arriving at all."

—*Lost Horizon*

I met Zhongdian's governor Qi Zhala, an ethnic Tibetan. To my surprise, he was dressed not as a cadre in Western tie and jacket, but as an ordinary Tibetan in a long dark robe. Unlike other officials in China, he made no pretension of who he was because he knew his roots.

Sitting casually on a wooden bench between log and wooden buildings in the old section of Zhongdian, which he sought to save and preserve, Qi Zhala seemed casual, perfectly at home in his hometown. He presided over what the central government has now proclaimed as "Shangri-La County".

Pointing at the dirt road running between wooden buildings, which could have been a set from a Western movie, I asked, "Is this a street in the Tea Caravan Trail?"

"Yes," he replied briskly. "The Tea Caravan Trail ran from Simao

and Pu'er to Dali, Lijiang, Zhongdian; over the mountains to Chamdo and Lhasa; and eventually to India and Nepal. Throughout the Ming and Qing dynasties, this was a major trade route. During those days, when caravans plied the mountains, Zhongdian was an important station on the route."

"Is that why you wish to preserve the old town of Zhongdian?" I asked. "Other cities in China are busy destroying their old sections, obliterating their own heritage in the name of development. What do you want to achieve?"

Qi Zhala explained, "The ancient city of Zhongdian has heritage value that must be preserved. This city dates from the Tang Dynasty and as a trade station, it was also a center for multi-cultural integration between Tibetan, Hans, Naxi and Bai. Architectural heritages merged and many of the old cities of the Qinghai-Tibetan Plateau are already gone. Aside from Barkor in

heritage," explained Qi Zhala. "Moreover, it is our intention to protect the environment. The local people support it and our planning departments have decided to protect it comprehensively."

"This represents really progressive innovation compared to anywhere in China," I ventured. "What about Beijing, the nation's capital? Is the plan in raising the old city for the Olympics and leaving a few Chinese facades like movie sets destroying everything of heritage value?"

"We think differently," Qi Zhala nodded with confidence. "The old should be kept old, and it should be preserved with cultural protection as the central objective. Some cities use just superficial cultural motifs by tearing down the old city and replacing it with steel and cement structures. This creates something from what it was originally. We have chosen a separate path — to protect the old heritage because history is continuity. Preserving our culture within is true heritage protection."

"You are really a leader — pioneering heritage protection in China."

"There are other examples of cities that are well preserved," Qi Zhala added graciously. "Lijiang and Dali are such examples. We want to study the successful examples and avoid the mistakes of other cities. Moreover, our intention is not to just commercially exploit the old city, but carefully protect the architectural heritage and preserve our culture through this process."

"Most cities in China are just cement structures covered with bathroom tiles and blue glass. The whole country seemed to be fixated with Freudian bathroom fixtures for external decoration. Zhongdian has not done this. Why?"

"This was a group decision of ours," Qi Zhala admitted. "We already started doing this, but we recognized the problem early and we are determined to tear down the tiles and blue glass, creating a Tibetan look for the new city structures using original materials. It is not just face-masking the city, but reviving the original Tibetan architectural style and heritage in the new city. As for the old city, it will not be touched."

"But how will you address technical infrastructure needs for the old city?"

"We want to have a traditional, cultural city. Our city may appear ancient, but we have electricity, water, and modern facilities. But where we have the ancient culture, it should be protected."

"This effort will in turn protect the environment surrounding the old city, won't it?"

"Shangri-La is a rare ecosystem zone," Qi Zhala explained, "with an enormous diversity of environment, ecology and culture. So it needs to be protected. Protecting the environment, architecture and traditional culture and the supporting sectors is an integrated effort. Forests,

waters, and mountains need accelerated protection measures that also involve fighting pollution and garbage. We will not allow plastic bags and anything alien to affect the environment. Even on the use of agricultural pesticides, we have very strict guidelines as to what can be used so as not to destroy the soil or have any adverse spin-off effects."

"Your approach is so different from Beijing's," I pointed out, "where the city government, in the name of rapid development, not only obliterated its cultural heritage but has turned the city into an environmental disaster unsuitable for human beings to live in."

"We feel our environment is part of our human heritage," Qi Zhala replied. "We must protect it and the culture that is an integral

part of it. Actual protection of forest and ecology is interrelated with the protection of the culture. If you do not have blue skies and green mountainsides, then there is no Shangri-La. If you do not have traditional culture, then the ecology misses its spirit. Actually, protecting ethnic people's culture in its traditional form naturally protects the environment."

"Are you saying by protecting Tibetan culture," I asked, "Tibetans by nature will in turn protect the environment because that, in itself, is integral to their culture?"

"When we talk about ecological protection, we must talk about our Tibetan culture," Qi Zhala emphasized. "We Tibetans herd animals,

155

which is a traditional occupation in conflict with industrial development. We do not need industrial development here in Zhongdian. We have selected sectors to develop, such as traditional herding, agriculture and crafts. We do not want the kind of industrial development that will destroy our ecosystem. People and nature should be in close relationship and should not be in conflict. Nature is not to be destroyed or we will destroy ourselves. Shangri-La may only be an ideal from a philosophical perspective, but a place where humanity and environment are in harmony and spirituality exceeds materialism can be achieved."

"Is your approach in conflict with China's established development model — measuring success based on GDP growth, as well as on how much cement and steel can be churned into real estate projects, or on how many fancy big cars can choke the streets?"

"Real development involves protection," Qi Zhala was emphatic. "Recognizing and protecting what is really important represents true development. Actually, ecological protection is a sector unto itself. This sector fits our traditional lifestyle and our own region. We have chosen it. The total picture of development is not just high-rise buildings and smoke stacks. Sure, you can urbanize yourselves, but this does not necessarily mean you are developed. Development is not only large-scale industrialization. We have over 300,000 people here. We see development in a larger perspective. Protecting our mountains, forests and lifestyle is development for us."

White Horse Buddha

"We are all glad to see you, though the meeting is almost as puzzling as the fact of us being here at all. Indeed, we were just about to make our way up to your lamasery, so it is doubly fortunate. If you could give us directions for the journey..."

—*Lost Horizon*

I took the bus from Zhongdian to Deqin, following rivers cutting into canyons. The road seemed long, and the air became thinner as the bus zigzagged up mountain passes. The altitude rose like a cloud, evoking the feeling of anticipation in finding something that was always there.

Looking down the road into sheer red canyons, I could feel vomit erupting through my throat as dizziness preceded conscious realization that the truck was swirling around a hairpin bend in the road. The road was washed out but teeters upon gravel that fell delicately like rain-drops into the canyon. I held back the vomit with my right hand so that other passengers in the bus would not notice. Approaching 4,000 meters, I was beginning to feel altitude sickness. To balance the senses, I stared into the canyon, a parallel extremity between river and earth. Nobody was in it.

Ravens cried. They laughed at me and then danced away in the wind. The presence of wind was momentary. It too will be gone, but might return. One thing became certain — the ravens were here first — they would return after I had left.

Eventually, past a hairpin curve in the road, we arrived at the White Horse Mountain — its peak covered with distant snow, framed in violet purple flowers, yellow in the grass, among short pines scratching the cuff of my jeans. At this altitude, the flowers never fade. They pass in sequence before time and perpetuate in the space provided by the thin air.

Passing nomads were sitting before blue-and-white patterned Tibetan tents. They just sat there playing chess in the afternoon, oblivious to my presence. The sun crossed from behind the shoulder of one nomad, illuminating black and white chess pieces upon a checkered board, and then descended behind the shoulder of another. The nomads were oblivious to the passing of sunlight between them as well.

They had always been oblivious to the presence of others who had come and gone before me. So I thought, why should I be different? I was on my way somewhere where they had been before, only to return once again when the seasons change and the summer air fills with snow. One drank, another laughed, as the third played a two-stringed Tibetan mandolin. I stopped and asked them where Shangri-La was. They looked at me as if I had gone mad, which reminded me that I had already answered my own question.

In fact, I was just chasing a feeling of calm that was sustained in the shortness of breath at 4,200 meters above sea level. At this altitude, even walking slowly brought on intermediate acute headaches. Coffee would not help. As I pissed out the morning's cup of coffee at 4,200 meters, I could feel the emptiness of warm urine evaporating before touching earth.

The Tibetans told me, if I prostrate to the mountain three times,  clouds will pass and reveal its peak. Burn pine incense, and remember to hold the smell of its purity burning to heaven in your mind, and dream of clouds passing before the mountains.

I stopped before prayer flags draped in zigzags across a crest of mountain, where the road turned sharply. I sat and stared at the

blue sky through the prayer flags. Realization occurred that I was dreaming with the mountains.

Workers had fixed the sign marking the bend in this road and the crevice of the mountain pass. It read 4,200 meters. I asked to borrow their red paintbrush. I painted it red and then walked away.

But I did not walk very far. I came upon a stout man in a yellow silk shirt, wrapped in the red robes of a lama. Like the mountain, his name was White Horse. In fact, he was the Rimpoche "White Horse Buddha". I asked him for directions.

"Yes, this is the Tea Caravan Trail," he responded. "It is sometimes called 'the road to Shangri-La'."

"There seem to be sacred mountains along the whole route?"

"Of course, the Cang Mountain of Dali, the Jade Dragon Mountain

of Lijiang, the Haba Mountain and the White Horse Mountain are all sacred to the indigenous people of each place. The trail and mountains along it will eventually bring you to Kawagebo. It is the most important in the chain of Yunnan sacred mountains. It is the high point of the Tea Caravan Trail before you leave Yunnan and enter Tibet."

"What is in Kawagebo?" I asked. "What will I find climbing it?"

"There are Dakinis living there. They float and can appear anywhere at any time. In some places, you can see stones used by them as tools for cooking. Pilgrims to the mountain often make little houses with stone so that spirits of the deceased returning to the mountain can have a place to live in the mountain as well."

"Stones?"

"Yes," he replied assuredly. "You will see a large stone there. It was blessed by the Karmapa as part of a Karma Kadju ceremony. Beyond the stone is the Lotus Temple. It marks the highest point you can attain."

"Ok," I questioned. "All along the Tea Caravan Trail are these sacred mountains. What makes them different from other mountains? What makes them sacred?"

"The concept of a sacred mountain involves not just the mountain, but also the mountain surrounding the spirit within. The source is Buddha. Beneath Buddha are the Bodhisattvas, followed by the Taras and Dakinis. The sacred mountains are connected with Buddhism. They are places where the Bodhisattvas and Dakinis can descend to earth."

"Frankly, I have been following the Tea Caravan Trail looking for Shangri La. Some said it would be in Duli, then Lijiang. Now some say it is here in Diqing. Where is Shangri-La?"

"It is within. Actually Shangri-La is Shambhala. In Tibetan Buddhism, the king of Shambhala lives in a realm between the sun and the moon within each person. The question of where it is cannot be answered the way you might anticipate. It is something you feel but cannot say, because it goes beyond words."

"Can you lamas go there?"

"High level lamas can be in Shambhala at any time. They can go there in their dreams. But they can also be anywhere at anytime. It is a state of mind, not matter, because their level of meditation has reached this height of consistency. Some people say Shambhala is north of here, near the border of India and Tibet. Others say it is above a snow-capped mountain. Actually, it is an internal factor, not external."

"What is it like?"

"It is described as a place surrounded by snow-capped mountains and calm lakes. Within the center is a lotus flower. Within the lotus is an ultimate space that cannot be crossed. Within it is a realm that is void of fightings, diseases, and sicknesses."

"Have you ever been there?"

"During meditation, I have been able to feel in the separation of my soul from body such a place. To dream is only to dream. Through meditation in a state of calm, I have felt that place. I felt a valley of lotus between the snow-capped mountains. It is a place most people cannot go to. But within the mountain range, there are springs, flowers and grass. Animals like bears, wolves, wild rabbits and peacocks all live together without conflict. The main thing here is meditation. That is all everyone does. There are Tibetan lamas and Taoist teachers. There is such a place. I believe what I visited is just a corner of the periphery entering Shambhala."

"So by following this route, can I get there?"

"I believe you will eventually get there. Not because you follow this route, but because you have decided to take the first step by following it. It will not bring you there, but the intention to take this step will. Remember, an ideal is empty. Many people say, 'Well it's empty, so there is nothing there.' But because it is empty, it is free from the material. In this, there is much to discover."

KAWAGEBO

You will return to the mountain one day
in your subconscious at a point to be
arrived at,
only when you finally cease to remember.

I arrived in Deqin at night. It is a small cowboy town around 3,600 meters above sea revel. This makes it at the same altitude as Lhasa. The air here is cold and fresh. Beyond Deqin is another narrow, curving road. It leads past Tibetan teahouses toward Kawagebo — one of the most sacred mountains in the Tibetan chain.

The whole region is soaked in tales of Kawagebo.Once a demonic monster who terrorized the villages, Kawagabo was conquered and

168

transformed into a protector spirit by the great tantric master Padmasambhava. The spirit remains in the mountain, making Kawagebo one of the important protector mountains for Tibetans.

In this simple tale is a fundamental core power of Tibetan philosophy — negative energy can be turned around by positive, if utilized correctly.

Known as the "Lotus-Born Master", Padmasambhava is historically credited as having brought Buddhism to Tibet sometime in the 8th Century AD. An adept miracle worker, he travelled across the Himalayan region teaching tantric practice, and turning demons into protectors. He taught the power of using one's mind to turn positive into negative. Nearly all branches of Tibetan Buddhism originate from this unique legendary yogic master who is considered by Tibetans as the second Buddha.

Kawagebo as the protector mountain, is worshiped in many ways. Throughout Deqin, monasteries and shrines contain statues of Kawagebo, depicting the protector spirit as a fierce general, riding a white horse. Pilgrims circumambulate the mountain or climb to the Lotus Temple to honor Padmasambava, and hang prayer flags called longda to spread positive energy to others. A pilgrimage to Kawagebo reminds those taking the journey of the power of one's thoughts. A single positive action can reverse a chain of negative ones. It all begins with one's own intention.

It is said that Dakinis dwell in the mountain. They can fly to the highest point of blue in heaven and back again within a split second. They are not restrained by any of the constraints we tend to place on time and space. They can break through barriers conceived in our own minds and shatter assumptions. Time and space is a construct that consist of only our own limited assumptions concerning that which is beyond what we already know.

Kawagebo is a mysterious mountain. In the Himalayan chain, it is not really considered all that high as a mountain. In fact, there are many mountains much higher. But for some reason, it cannot be climbed. All expeditions that had been attempted to reach its summit were met with disaster. A memorial of a joint Chinese-Japanese team of experienced professional mountain climbers stands near the eight pagodas, marking

the main viewing point of the mountain. None of the climbers survived.

Today, local villagers dissuade climbers for their own safety. The whole point is that a spirit mountain is not meant to be climbed but worshiped. We should not think about conquering nature, but rather respecting it.

There is however, a pilgrimage route up the side of the mountain. It leads from the town of Minyong at the base of Kawagebo, up past the Prince Temple, to the Lotus Temple. This is the highest point, which stops at a ravine near the glaciers. From here, one can stare at the white in afternoon sunlight. If one listens quietly, one can hear the sound of glaciers melting.

Temple Where Buddha Flew

"Deep below them the valley of the Blue Moon was like a cloud, and to Conway the scattered roofs had a look of floating after him in the haze."

—*Lost Horizon*

A winding road leads up from the cowboy town of Deqin toward the sacred Tibetan mountain Kawagebo. Along the way are roadside teahouses. Many are built of wood and old logs fitted together with packed dirt. They sell yak butter tea and flat Tibetan bread to pilgrims making the climb.

"Is a cup of tea the only thing you want?" whispered a voice from a darkness that was illuminated by a single yak butter candle in a crevice of the wall. I could barely see the shadow of her voice.

"No, actually I am looking for directions," I replied. Her form became clearer as my eyes adjusted to the candlelight

"Are you also making pilgrimage to Kawagebo?" she asked with a hint of disbelief.

"Yes. That's why I stopped here. I heard there is a temple near here called the Temple Where Buddha Flew. I am looking for the temple."

"You may be looking too hard," she said with a sarcastic whisper. "It is just up the road. To reach the temple from the roadside, there is a long path of prayer wheels. When turning each wheel, do so with deliberation. That means slowly. Then you can find what you are looking for."

She crouched in the darkness, one leg folded under her small frame. She leaned on the other knee just under her chin. She was wrapped in a frayed jacket of bright nomadic colors. Her hair was tied above her head, exposing curving silver earrings and a silver stud that punctured the skin under her lower lip, another in her nose, giving her the presence of half an Indian Hari Krishna and half a punk rocker.

She seemed like a young nomad in disguise.

"What's your name?" I asked.

"Blue Moon. I am named after a valley."

Not sure whether she was a pilgrim or a hippie, I quickly concluded
she was a gypsy. "Valley of the Blue Moon is the name of the location
where Shangri-la is said to exist, at least according to Hilton's novel
'Lost Horizon.'" I then asked in a low voice, "How did you get a name like
that?"

"Think ofthe moon when it is full and there are no clouds. That is
the time when you can see things the clearest. It is the mood of blue
when one is meditating on the river by listening to the sound emanating

from water passing rocks. Eventually the rocks will erode, even disappear. But the water will continue to change its form. Because water has no form. It is limitless. But changes in the position of the moon can change the pattern of ripples in water."

"So what are you doing here? Are you a pilgrim going to Kawagebo?"

"I am returning to the mountain. By the way, the temple you asked about, it is just up the road. We can go there."

175

Together, we wandered up a bend in the road. From it, a row of prayer wheels led to the temple. We turned the wheels. She led me to the temple.

"It is called the Temple Where Buddha Flew," she explained. "Local Tibetans tell of a time in their not-so-distant past, before they could remember, but not really that long ago. That time was a moment."

"What does a moment have to do with a flying Buddha?" I asked incredulously.

"It was the moment he flew," she said strikingly, as if my question was stupid. "It is amazing what can happen in just a single moment. Moments are like that, you know, they come and go and bring with them amazing feelings and memories, except most of the time we are too concentrated on trivia to grasp these things that are contained in a moment and bring them inside. The great Indian masters taught us that there is only past and future. The present does not exist. It is what we call a moment. But if you think about it, there is only the present. Because the past is gone but the future has not arrived. So we live always in a state of the present. But most of the time we are stuck on the past or worrying about the future. So the present passes us without being lived."

"Excuse me," I asked with insistence. "But can you explain how this moment is related to a flying Buddha? Are you saying that Buddha can fly at any moment and we should always be aware of this, and watching or something? Or is there a part of the puzzle I am not seeing?"

"Oh, you want to know what really happened during that moment a long time

ago. Right? Ok. I will tell you. This very compassionate
image of Buddha was once over there, on the other
side of a ravine full of sunflowers on a distant
mountainside," she pointed with an outstretched
finger, exposing an enormous round yellow amber
stone set into a silver ring. It rose from her
outstretched finger like a mountain. While her face
seemed young, her had was old. It was a hand that had worked hard. "One
day, the Buddha just flew across the ravine to this mountainside, and
stayed here. So our people built this temple around the Buddha. That's
why we call it the 'Temple Where Buddha Flew'. See what can happen in
a moment?"

"How sure are you of this story?" I asked cynically.

"How sure are you of what happens in any given moment?" she asked
with a smile that remained unrevealing, but most certain.

"I am not. You never can be."

"If you do not believe what I have said, then you should sit on
the hillside and watch yellow flowers glistening in the purity of the
afternoon sun and falling upon earth spreading like gold crystals. Then
you can begin to dream of Buddha's image flying across the ravine. Be
careful. You may fall asleep in the afternoon sun. If you become dizzy
staring at flowers turning gold, enter the darkness of the temple and
stare upon Buddha's eyes. Those eyes will ask you many questions about
yourself. The question is: can you answer them?"

The thought was disturbing. Maybe those questions could be
answered, maybe not. Maybe they had never been asked.

Knowing without knowing what I was thinking, she continued,
oblivious to my thoughts. "That's because you have never looked into
his eyes. Try it. You will find that they are brightly lit and then begin

to understand that there is nothing wrong with disbelieving what you think is logical. Because logic is only a tool used to order your mind. It should not be confused with clarity. Actually, the logic is what creates confusion."

"Isn't logic and clarity the same?"

She shook her head with a feeling of half disappointment and slight disregard for what really did not matter. Her oversized silver earrings dangled like parakeet cages shifting in a breeze as her head shook. "If you can avoid disorder, then the tool of logic like order itself becomes unnecessary. If your mind has found clarity, then you no longer need logic."

"Then how does one find clarity?"

"Go to the mountain."

Seeing the Mountain

"Conway could see the outline of a long valley, with rounded sad-looking hills on either side jet-black against deep electric blue of the night-sky. But it was to the head of the valley that his eyes were led irresistibly , for there, soaring into the gap, and magnificent to the full shimmer of moonlight, appeared what he took to be the most loveliest mountain on earth."

—*Lost Horizon*

Seeing the mountain

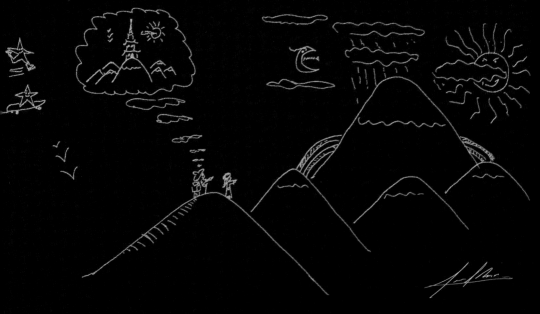

From the Temple Where Buddha Flew, we hitchhiked a ride on the back of a van toward Kawagebo. It dropped us off before another row of teahouses across from eight white pagodas which mark the main viewing point of Kawagebo.

But we could not see the mountain because the valley before was shrouded in late summer mist. Rising in heat from the afternoon sun, mist clustered, becoming clouds, veiling Kawagebo's face. All that could be seen of the mountains were clouds.

"It is the hardest to see the mountain in summer," Blue Moon explained. "This is because summer rains bring clouds. They obscure the mountain's pure white face. Sometimes, photographers come here and wait for weeks to see the mountain, but the spirit

Kawagebo refuses to show his face. That does not mean it cannot be seen, only that you cannot see it. The clouds just won't depart."

With a flick of her hand, which cling-clanged of silver bracelets descending from elbow to wrist, she led me into a small shrine by the roadside. Within it was the figure of a warrior protector spirit with a powerful face, arms holding weapons, and riding on a white horse. Blue Moon burned incense, then nodded at me to follow. "Pray for protection from Kawagebo. He is the protector spirit of our people and our mountain."

"A protector spirit?"

"Actually, he is the mountain."

"But who is he?" I asked, trying to make sense of it all. "Is he that protector spirit on the horse in the altar, or the mountain over there that we cannot see because it is covered with clouds?"

"The protector spirit is the mountain," Blue Moon explained. "But once, the mountain was a demon with nine heads and eighteen hands. The demon terrified people living in the villages. There was no way to appease him," she sighed with a shrug. "That was until the Indian 'Lotus-Born Master', Padmasambhava, who we Tibetans call Guru Rimpoche came. He was invited to Tibet in the eighth century by King Trisong Detsen to conquer demons obstructing the construction of the Samye Monastery. He conquered them and the monastery was built. After leaving Samye, he traveled throughout Tibet helping Tibetan people to overcome demons with his powers. Wherever there was a demon, he turned it into a mountain to protect the people. That is why we Tibetans have so many protector mountains, thanks to Guru Rimpoche, the 'Lotus-Born Master'." Then with another wave of her hand encrusted in turquoise and silver rings, she suggested, as if an afterthought, "Now it is time to prostrate before the mountain."

It suddenly occurred to me that the values we have been brought up with are maybe just statues to man's own cherished ego, like the big marble chunks of monuments in public parks photographed by lots of tourists every year. Tourists line up patiently to go through the security systems, but do not know what those statues symbolize, and do not practice the forgotten beliefs behind them. In the end, these monuments represent not a set of beliefs, but an expression of having lost touch with one's very self.

For a moment, images of my past life rushed into my mind. The things we were taught to believe may never have existed except in the news reports. Like commercials, they too were illusory — ultimately paid advertisers, multinational corporations that want you to believe in the things they sell you. The freedoms we believe in exist only within the confines of broadcast airwaves owned by government and licensed to those richer than us, who use them to sustain a system to their benefit. Actually, we cannot trust anybody in this Oz wizard game. Since Breton Woods, they have been creating a dysfunctional society based on a series of myths perpetuated through media monopoly, owned by corporations that are supported through the trading of debt instruments in a pyramid system that is an illussion and does not collapse only because we have been persuaded to believe in it. The last premise of our existence, the environment, will soon be the next to be taken away. When that is gone, we can probably live in air-conditioned shopping malls like space chips and thrive on brand consumerism and fast food until our bodies rot with diseases and the doctors, pharmaceutical companies, lawyers and insurance companies can collect their side of the bargain. Don't worry about the cost of human life or the desecration of our environment, as it will all be capitalized with the excesses written off as part of shareholder's value. In the end, we will all be classified as either a statistic or dividend.

My thoughts echoed the sound of clouds. I sat before Kawagebo waiting for clouds to pass. They began to depart. Before the natural splendor of Kawagebo, I was reminded that maybe mountains are not really meant to be conquered. Their foundations are the earth from which all things sprout, grow, leave and return. Maybe all along we have been forgetting this.

My silence was broken by the thoughts of ravens laughing in the wind. Blue Moon interrupted the caw of ravens entering my thoughts. She asked if I wanted to burn incense. She had already asked me several times, but I could not hear her. My mind had been carried away on the black feathers of raven laughter. She pointed to the wind — it was carrying incense to clouds. She reminded me that it was time to burn more incense.

She then broke branches of a pine tree possessing a scent rising in red colors. Feeding the branches into a white earthen burner, and taking a bottle of water, tossed a few drops onto the burning pine. Scented smoke drifted like sounds of a flute being played on a cloud somewhere above the point where senses occasionally withdraw to meet.

"Wander with me," she beckoned, leading clockwise around eight white pagodas. Prayer flags tied tightly together crisscrossed the footpath. We had to duck in some places and even crawl under the entanglement of prayer flags to circumambulate the eight pagodas.

She led me to a quiet place beyond the eight pagodas where the ground was somewhat worn. "Here, we prostrate before the sacred mountain Kawagebo," she whispered in a half-breath voice. Then disregarding my presence, touching clasped hands to the top of her head, forehead, throat and chest, in sequence without hesitation or even second thought, she bent down on all fours touching her head to the earth.

"These points represent the Buddha or enlightened one, the Dharma or teachings of Buddha, and the Sangha or community of Buddhists," she explained, raising both clasped hands again. She repeated the prostration three times. Without saying anything, I followed.

"These points also correspond to the chakras running through our bodies," she said as half an afterthought, rising after touching her forehead to the earth. Her long black hair had fallen, now shrouding her forehead like a veil. She shook it back and laid both eyes firmly on mine. "The chakras are points

linking mind and body. Energy flows from the top of
our heads to the bottom of our sexual organs, along
the line of chakras. To begin tapping into the energy
contained in our dark side, we must open the chakras
to find our light."

As she said this, with half a breath tasting like ice,
the sun appeared behind the clouds. Through the thickness
of clouds, it appeared as a disc of thin light. Imagine somebody placing
a candle behind a veil, which then melts before the candle. This was the
feeling of clouds parting. Rays of light pierced like descending arrows.
The whole Kawagebo mountain range emerged like an altar beneath
stained glass with warmth pouring from rains of light above as mists
dissolved into fragments of sunlight.

Pointing to the mountain, she whispered, "This is the feeling when
clouds depart."

Finding the Key

"The white pyramid in the distance compelled the mind's ascent as passionately as a Euclidean theorem, and when at last the sun rose into the sky of deep delphinimum blue, he felt only a little less than comfortable again."

—*Lost Horizon*

"Before entering Kawagebo," Blue Moon explained in her soft whispery voice, "you must find the key."

"The key?"

"The key."

"Sorry, but why do you need a key to go climb a mountain?"

"No, you need the key to open the mountain."

"Ok," I was puzzled. "So where do we go to get this key? Is there like a key-maker shop back in Deqin or some place like that where we have to go?"

"No," she shook her head slightly, revealing only the tiniest bit of frustration with my question. "The key is not available anywhere. It must be taken from a temple named Qi Deng Ge, which is known to few and can hardly be found unless you take a winding river road from Deqin and follow it until it reaches a river that must be crossed before coming to the temple. If you do not ask local Tibetans for directions, you will not find the temple. If you ask too persistently, they will not tell you."

"So the key is at the temple?"

"Before the pilgrimage to Kawaqebo, one must obtain the key," Blue Moon implored. "It can unlock the entrance to the mountain."

I thought about arriving at this temple to look for a key. I wondered whether it would be a large, wide-ringed key, whether it would fit into a lock, which would click with the prick of the point and creak when the door opens. I was soon to discover that such key is invisible, intangible, and inconceivable. In fact, the find the key it must be conceived in the mind. That was the whole point of going to the temple.

We crossed the river and approached the temple that appeared like a fairy castle made by dripping white sand. "There is no closed door except the subconscious mind," Blue Moon explained. "The key can open its inner recesses provided they are willing and ready to be opened. The

key can only be found by walking in perpetual circles around the temple. These are kora or circumambulations that calm the mind and bring more certainty to each step, with each step you take in the circumambulation. So the riddle in opening the door is not finding the key, but opening the circles."

I found this temple looked nothing like any ordinary temple visited before, because it does not look like a temple at all. It really looked like a sand castle — a white one. The temple was completely surrounded by protruding white stalagmite-looking formations made of plaster. They appeared like drip walls like those I made on sand flats at the beach as a kid,, or in terms of dimension, like enormous anthills found in Africa. After walking through the gate, we followed rows of drip sand castle walls. Air filled with burning incense from pine branches having just

touched fire kept alive by more pine branches in white earthen burners. Prayer flags fluttered in wind. Blue Moon reminded me, "Take a moment to observe the color of wind."

Aside from pilgrims beginning their journey to Kawagebo, there were older women and young schoolgirls from nearby villages hanging around the temple. They have no particular journey. Instead, they come to this temple every day, to sweep it clean and follow the

circumambulation route. They told us the history of this temple.

It is said that at a time which nobody can really quite remember, but which everybody is most certainly sure of, a crystal Buddhist pagoda was discovered here. To protect the pagoda, Tibetan pilgrims brought plaster and water and plastered the pagoda. They kept plastering it until they ended up with many plaster pagodas, one on top of another, one after another in a great circumference around the temple, until the entire place looked like a big plaster birthday cake. Then they forgot which plaster pagoda contained the buried crystal pagoda. But that became irrelevant. The important thing was the accumulated energy in this spot. That is why pilgrims arrive here first to get the key, before going to into the mountain.

The old women and young girls come every day to clean the pagodas, so the white plaster stayed white. They do this for the pilgrims. Then they follow the pilgrims.

"Forget about trying to look for the crystal pagoda," they explained. "It is here, that is all you need to know. Do you see all these pilgrims? These are people from nearby Deqin. They come here to add plaster to protect the crystal pagoda. It is a duty we must do, to care for its protection. In turn, if your intention is good and you come here and pray for something, you will get it."

Before entering Kawagebo, Tibetan pilgrims come and walk around the plaster fairy-like formations — like something out of Salvador Dali's imagination, when clocks stopped clicking and stretched to become shadows at sunset on horizons, reaching beyond places where horses and elephants fall apart. Here, they can be put precariously back together, sometimes with wings.

Within the temple chamber is an image of Buddha. You cannot photograph the image. The Tibetan women guarding the temple will tell you why. They will whisper in soft but persuasive voices that this image is especially powerful, so much so that those who photograph it will take away disaster. So do not photograph the Buddha. But other temples in the Tibetan regions do not have such strict concerns about photographing images. This is what makes this particular one especially different. But taking such photographs does not really matter at all. You realize that it is impossible anyways for a photograph to carry away the impression in your mind, which you will leave at this place when you depart.

"Those who come to find the key must do many kora circumambulations.". A lady guarding the shrine explained. "This is the only way to arrive upon the key. Here, you may follow the Tibetans and make requests for help, or seek answers to questions that are unresolved in your mind."

Circling the surrealistic white pagodas feels like something out of a Freudian dream. Freud understood that dreams are subconscious reality and conscious reality is often fragmented dreams. So dreams are sometimes more important than reality. Some people dream during the day and sleep at night.Some dream all day and all night, because there is no difference between day and night. Actually they are one.

"The knots. The knots. You have forgotten about the knot," Blue Moon interrupted my daydreaming."If you stop dreaming, then

you can no longer untie the knots.By circling the temple, unresolved knots in your mind may become untied, threads unwoven. That is what I meant by 'finding the key'. Comprehending dissolution on horizons means obtaining the key before entering the mountain. Look," she pointed with a long outstretched arm dangling with silver bracelets. "Can you see the shadows dissolving into the sunset?"

"I cannot see a thing. This whole valley seems surrounded by mountains. So how can you see beyond the shadows if the sun is behind the mountain?"

"That is because you are not looking to the horizon," she laughed.

Moving Clouds

"He was also interested in the mountain beyond the valley;
it was a sensational peak, by any standards, and he was
surprised that some traveler had not made much of it in the
kind of book that a journey in Tibet invariably elicits. He
climbed it in mind as he gazed, choosing a route by col and
couloir until an exclamation from Mallison drew his attention
back to earth...'You were contemplating the mountain, Mr.
Conway?' came the enquiry."

—*Lost Horizon*

After finding the key to the mountain, we returned to the eight white pagodas facing Kawagebo at dawn the next morning. Blue Moon was insistant that we awake early. She had heard that eight Rimpoche, would be giving prayers before the mountain at dawn. A Rinpoche – which means "precious jewel" in Tibetan -- is a reincarnated lama, in Chinese huo fuo or "living Buddha." To have eight Rinpoche arrive at Kawagebo to say prayers was a special moment. Even before dawn many local Tibetans were arriving for the occassion.

Sure enough, the eight Rinpoche arrived in a van and stood before eight white pagodas lined up before eight peaks of the Kawagebo range. The eight Rinpoche came to burn pine incense. One could not see any of the peaks of Kawagebo because of the clouds. Blue Moon said with a whisper, "They came to part the clouds."

Recitations of prayer rang like chimes of caravan pony bells across a valley not yet awakened from the perfumed sound of mist.

Mist and clouds inseparable, the eight Rinpoche began pouring holy

water from plastic bottles of iced tea. Blue Moon said it would part the clouds. I could not see the connection between throwing out iced tea and dissipating clouds, I asked her to explain.

"It is said that many years ago, the Tenth Panchen Lama came to this same place and used a can of Coca Cola, turning it into holy water and making clouds part before the sacred mountain. At the time, many journalists came and took photos of Panchen Lama as he stood before Kawagebo."

One black and white photo was stuck to a raw wooden post of the teahouse we sat in that morning, waiting for the eight Rinpoche to arrive, eating Tibetan zamba and drinking yak butter tea. That was when she told me the story about turning Coke into holy water. Tibetans might think of it as a miracle; to multinationals, a globalization victory. I stared at the photo. Panchen Lama's hands were folded behind his back as he stood facing the camera. I could not see any can of Coke. Clearly, they overlooked an advertising opportunity.

I was skeptical about all this talk of turning commercial soft drinks into holy water until the eight Rinpoche got out of their van. Standing amidst the clouds shrouding the eight white pagodas, they recited chants holding aloft holy zamba — barley cereal. Sure enough, clouds separated with the smoothness of a velvet curtain dragging across a

London stage, pausing half open, half closed, exposing the sharp white peak of Kawagebo in a clarity of freshness, which became clearest in the morning.

For a moment, I thought the mountain, like an actor, would bow. Hands aloft in deference to Kawagebo, it seemed as if the mountain had given the eight "Living Buddhas" respect by opening its clouds to their prayers. They tossed zamba, which become sacred grains upon leaving their hands. They tossed them everywhere. The wind blew. The zamba departed into fine airborne grains that could not be seen by anyone. The ravens cawed.

Clouds parted, exposing the peak. The eight Rinpoche gave blessing to those who gathered, and thanks to the spirit of the mountain. The eight Rinpoche then left in the same rickety van they arrived in. Clouds passed like boats floating at sea, and Kawagebo once again shrouded itself in mist.

I was mesmerized and would never have believed this if I had not seen it myself. But I had. This moment fundamentally changed my perception of what it means to believe. Mental concentration can burn mist; maybe even raise Coke stock prices.

"It is now time for you to begin your pilgrimage to Kawagebo," Blue Moon remindedme with a breathy whisper. "Only this way can you begin to understand how power in the belief of your own thoughts can move clouds."

Entering the Mountain

"He gazed over the edge into the blue-black emptiness.
The drop was phantasmal; perhaps as much as a mile. He
wondered if he would be allowed to descend it and inspect
the valley civilization that had been talked of."

—*Lost Horizon*

Entering the Mountain

The journey into Kawagebo begins not up, but down. Roads wind along cliffs, leading through a valley and arriving at the Lancang River, which flows south, eventually becoming the Mekong, nourishing Southeast Asia.

I thought about the people living in houses on stilts wearing bandannas, which I had seen as a young boy flipping through National Geographic. I thought about how they drank the same water flowing from snows melting from glaciers of Kawagebo. In fact, there are three rivers running parallel around this sacred mountain — the Yangtze, the Mekong, and the Ganges — ultimately connecting China, Southeast Asia, and India at this spot. Kawagebo rests central on this spot. It would seem that the sources of three of the world's greatest civilizations flowed from mountain glaciers here, or that the mountain serves as an anchor point for the three great rivers. So before entering Kawagebo, we crossed the Mekong River.

Arriving at the base of Kawagebo, we were stopped at a roadblock beside a temple. Soldiers manned the roadblock. They were oblivious to the temple. The soldiers were there to protect the mountain as this was deemed an "environmentally protected zone". They wanted to register the license number of the jeep we were traveling in. We stopped. One soldier peered into the opened window of the vehicle. He spoke to the driver, warned him about damaging the environment, and told us not to take any wood or stones from the mountain.

At this point Blue Moon got off the vehicle turned to me and whispered, "To come here and take away a stone, or a piece of wood as souvenir, is useless," with an almost sarcastic disdain. "In fact, it is pointless." Then she added as half an afterthought before returning to her village."Go to the mountain with your heart and leave it there instead."

"Leave your heart? Where?On the mountain? How?" I called out to her.

"By connecting with the mountain,"Blue Moon laughed, turning to wander down the pathway leading to her village at the base of Kawegabo.

"How does one connect with a mountain?"

"Begin by having a conversation with the mountain."

The driver was busy registering the vehicle. He clearly was not interested in talking with mountains, it took time because the soldiers wanted him to fill out a piece of paper. There were other drivers waiting to fill out the same type of paper too. They were all very busy with broken pencils. So in the din of pencil scratching, I hopped off the vehicle and walked around three manidui placed between this temple and an ancient cedar tree, and thought about this talking with mountain stuff. The cedar had many white hada prayer scarves wrapped around it. I stopped before the tree, wondered how these scarves came to be wrapped around the tree, and then noticed Tibetan pilgrims each touching it with outstretched hands and foreheads in deference. Why the deference?

They stopped for a moment and told me, "When building the Samye Temple in Tibet nearly a millennium ago, many woodcutters invaded this valley, cutting down trees for money. They hoped to sell the wood to contractors building the Samye Temple. A rabbit came here and surprised the woodcutters because he could talk. Lying to them, he claimed to bring news from Tibet, saying the temple was already finished. Believing it, the workers stopped felling trees and went home. The rabbit laughed, running into the forest, kicking his paws in the air. In truth, the Samye Temple was still not built and was only in the middle of construction. But this smart rabbit had fooled the workers into dropping their axes, and so the cedar trees throughout this valley were saved. They continued to grow." Today, pilgrims tie hada around these same trees. They tied some more, and then left.

Upon hearing this story, I also touched the fine paper-thin bark of this magnificent cedar tree and thought that it might very well be 800 years old, or even older. Regardless, the message in this parable was clear as crystal river water of the Yangtze flowing before the tree. In Tibetan philosophy, it seemed more important to save trees than build temples.There is no need to build a temple just to believe in Buddhism. Better to protect trees.

Beside the tree, a temple had been built to honor the Lotus-Born Master,   the "second Buddha" whom Tibetans call Guru Rimpoche. A   Tibetan named Senla Duji had built it. I met him. He was there. In fact, after building the temple, he stayed there every day, and never left. As I stepped through the temple entrance, he just stood there. Staring with a smiling gentle face, he offered to show us the temple.

This did not take long, because the temple was very small.

But Senla Duji is a pretty big man. Once a famed hunter, his hunting prowess for killing so many animals spread like legend throughout all neighboring Tibetan valleys. Senla Duji was once quite proud of all his trophies. Then one day, he ventured up the mountain hunting, stopped suddenly, and faced his own reflection like a mirror in the side of the mountain. It is amazing how egos crack when one is forced to stare at one's own reflection.

Shocked by such strange phenomena, he wrote a letter to the Chinese Academy of Social Sciences in Beijing relating the occurrence, asking for a logical and scientific explanation as to why that had happened. There must be a logical, scientific reason why somebody suddenly sees his reflection in the side of a mountain. However, none of the academics at the Academy could explain. In the end, Senla Duji just dismissed the whole thing. Then he started to lose sleep. Soon, he could not sleep at all.

Every night, all the animals he had killed came to Senla Duji in his sleep, growling and threatening to bite him. He could hear them at his bedside every night, growling and howling. He could not sleep. So one morning, after a sleepless night, Senla Duji returned to the mountain, to that exact place where he had once seen his reflection. He asked the mountain what was really happening.

"These are the animals you have killed," explained Kawagebo incredulously. "Can't you see that? Don't you recognize them?"

Upon recognizing the reality of his own conscious acts, Senla Duji went mad. He climbed to a ridge above the Yangtze and hurled his gun into the river. He then picked up his ferocious hunting dog and threw him into the river as well. He frantically followed the river running past the base of Kawagebo, to this place beside the ancient cedar tree.

Here, he discovered the tree wrapped in hada.

Then he built a temple devoted to Padmasambhava, the Lotus-Born Master. It has since become the first stop of pilgrims entering Kawagebo on their way up the mountain to the Lotus Temple — the final point of pilgrimage — the highest point one can climb to. Now Senla Duji stays at his temple, reminding pilgrims passing, "Always respect mountains, and all lives — animals and plants — living in the mountains."

Ascending the Mountain

"But the next stage, though occassionally exciting, was less ardurous then we had prepared for., and a relief from the lung-bursting strain of the ascent. The track consisted of a traverse cut along the flank of a rock wall whose height above them the mist obscurred."

———-*Lost Horizon*

Upon receiving clearance, the vehicle drove to Minyong village at the base of the mountain. The village consists only of about six shops and teahouses. At Minyong, the road ends. There is no other way to climb up the mountain except to hike, or ride a horse. The vehicle stopped. We went looking for horses.

Tibetans living in Minyong operate a horse caravan running up to the Prince Temple, which is halfway up the mountain. You can find the caravan by walking on a trail that leads away from Minyong toward the mountain. Just listen for the sound of horse bells. They tinkle in the breeze and sound like water touching cold shiny rocks in a river that comes from the glaciers. Ponies cross the river. It is icy cold, even in summer. The cold is the disintegration of glaciers. Follow the sound of horse bells. They tinkle.

The tinkle of horse bells led up the mountain. In the stillness of the ancient forest, one could hear only the jingle of horse bells. If you did not know they were horses and listened to the jingle echo against the stillness captured in shadows of ancient cedar trees, you might just imagine their tinkle is the sound of Dakinis spirits who live in the mountain. Their voices can be faintly heard against the call of rivers rushing. If you listen to the power of river water pouring from glacier into the valley, and concentrate on the sound of glaciers disintegrating, maybe you can hear them.

The riverleads to Nang Wa Qu Guo, a place above the river. Here, it is said that one can see the reflections of sun and moon when the sky is clear and the sound of blue is green. This is because the river's water is believed to evolve from heaven. This belief is sustained by the fact that it comes from snows melting at the top of the mountain. The journey into Kawagebo begins by following the path of melting snow.

Deft pony hooves climbed the sharp bends in the trail. Their hooves

were almost delicate in their certainty. They stole moments in the journey to snip a chomp of grass.

A manidui called "A Ma Dumu" (the mother Tara) rises from the grass. There are many stones piled upon each other with the mantra, "Om Mani Bemi Hom", carved on them. Such stones were first placed upon this place centuries ago by a man in honor of his mother — an old lady who had come to climb Kawagebo. She had died on the way.

She collapsed at this place where mani stones are piled high. Following her footprints to the spot where she died, her son placed prayer stones on her shadow, releasing her spirit. To her, fulfilling life

meant completing the pilgrimage to Kawagebo. But she died halfway up the mountain. So her son came here, fulfilling her wish to complete the pilgrimage. He left the stones. Others came to share the wish. The pile grew higher as the years and pilgrims passed.

Resting in the shade, Tibetan pilgrims stopped as well. They shared another story told and retold among Tibetans in the region. The story is about a woman who was blind. Throughout her entire life, she had dreamt of making a pilgrimage to the holy city of Lhasa. But because she was blind, she could not make the trip.

Then one day, her son told her that he was going on a pilgrimage to Lhasa. This old blind woman was ecstatic. She asked her son to bring back just an ordinary stone from Lhasa. For her, in this life, it would be enough. Her son promised to fulfill the task.

In those days, the trip to Lhasa was long and arduous. The woman sat at home, waiting for her son to return. Three years passed. One day, as her son returned, recognizing the trail leading to his home, he remembered that he had forgotten to bring a stone from Lhasa to his poor blind mother.

Realizing how sad the old woman would be to learn that her son had forgotten her only wish, he picked up a stone from the front yard of their own home as he approached it. Then cleverly, he wrapped the stone in a hada prayer scarf. Upon entering his home, he presented his blind mother with the rock. Lying, he told her he had brought it all the way from Lhasa.

She was ecstatic, and placed it on her altar, prostrated before it and prayed. Because she was blind, she never realized that the stone was from her own front yard. Over time, it gradually transformed into an ocean conch shell. The conch shell is a sacred treasure in the pantheon of Tibetan Buddhist symbols. Lamas use conch shells as horns to announce the victory of compassion and wisdom over greed and ignorance.

The point of this story is to remind us all that even the stone in your own back yard can turn into treasure, if your heart is in the right place. Maybe you do not need to make the pilgrimage at all, if your intention is right. It is in your mind. By making a pilgrimage, you are not going on a physical journey either, but rather disconnecting all of the fragments of your life and placing them back together in the right way. The physical journey is only to force your mind to undertake pilgrimage.

I left the pile of prayer stones and followed the trail to a point where it winds past a huge tree called "Kang Gong Ba". In olden

times, a Tibetan landlord purchased the already ancient tree for himself because it was so big.

He then paid monks to pray and bless the tree. The landlord believed this tree possessed his family line. So the tree could not be cut or damaged. This is why he paid monks to bless it. The tree still stands today. One might wonder why somebody with as many material possessions as a landlord would want to buy a tree and have it blessed to protect his family line. Material wealth lacks roots.

Beyond the tree is a rock. Its name is "Dang Jing Pai Ba". "Under the rock lives Dang Jing, the guardian blacksmith, who makes horseshoes for the spirit Kawagebo, who rides a long-mane spirited white horse that neighs in the wind when rain becomes snow. Tibetan pilgrims on the route explained that the blacksmith Dang Jing is the doorman of Kawagebo. He opens his door every year on March 15th, when spring has arrived and the moon is bright. That day, the people from villages around Deqin burn incense for Kawagebo. In the burnt ashes, the old and wise can read the destiny of their village for the year ahead.

It is said that by leaning over and placing your ear close to the rock, one can hear faint sounds of the guardian blacksmith's bellows. But most people do not bother to lean over and those who do cannot necessarily hear the sound through a rock, because their own thoughts are rushing in circles like a whirlpool. The sound of a whirlpool is the movement of a river in convulsion. This is not the sound of a rock. To hear the sound of a rock, you must stop listening to convulsion. Then try and begin listening to the rock.

Here, the trail winds along cliffs looking over the river, which rushes past below, it drowns the sound of the rocks below, caught in current splitting the ravine.

There is a local story about two village boys who grew up together.

After growing up, they lived on different sides of the ravine. One became a lama, the other a hunter. Every day, the lama meditated; while every day, the hunter killed lots of animals and ate them, and sold their fur for money.

One day, the hunter suddenly realized the futility and evil of killing so many animals. Disheartened, he threw his money into the ravine and jumped off the mountain to his death. Enlightened upon dying, he became a Buddha.

The lama meditating on the other mountain looked across the ravine and was furious. The hunter had lived a life of killing and pleasure, but upon committing suicide, he became a Buddha. The lama was quite jealous. He had spent a life of frugality, meditating on the mountain in hopes of becoming an enlightened Buddha. If it was so easy to just jump off the mountain and become an enlightened Buddha upon death, he thought, then why not try committing suicide as well? He jumped and died, but did not become a Buddha.

The starting point of everything is your intention. The lama did not become enlightened because his intention was to become a Buddha. It was too deliberate. The hunter had lived a wrong life, but he realized this, awakened to it and changed his course of action. Action follows intention. If your intention is not positive, regardless of your action, the result will not be beneficial to anyone. But if your intention is positive, it can reverse the negative.

The Blind Man and the Temple

"He lay in this room, my dear Conway, where he could see from the window the white blur that was all his failing eyesight gave him of Karakal; but he could see with his mind also, he could picture the clear and matchless outline that he had first glimpsed half a century before."

—*Lost Horizon*

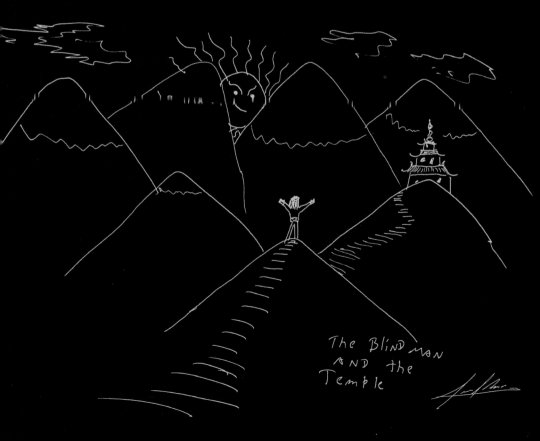

The Blind Man
AND the
Temple

Ascending through alpine forest, freshness rose from ice dissolving into water, crashing in white swirls among rocks in the ravine below. Mist arose when water dissipated. Mist drifted to linger on branches of ancient pines, rising with the mountain. The caravan followed a narrower trail among pine trees and entered the mist — by rising with the mountain.

When mist departs, it unveils clear shrill space, the distance between earth and sky, the mountain as protrusion of earth. In a clearing was grass. There stood horses. They were resting between caravans, eating grass. Behind the horses was the Prince Temple.

For Tibetans, Qoomolangma or Mount Everest, the world's highest precipice, is the "Mother Mountain". But Kawagebo is the "Prince". Its peak rises 6,740 meters above sea level, which makes it the smallest snow-capped mountain in the world. However, unlike Mount Everest, it cannot be climbed. In 1991, a Chinese-Japanese expedition tried to scale the mountain. All seventeen members died. To this day, nobody tries to climb Kawagebo.

Other expeditions have been stopped from climbing it, blocked by Tibetans living in nearby villages. They understand the riddle of a sacred mountain. Its peak cannot be climbed. Professional climbers have been so disappointed, because we have always been taught that mountains are to be conquered. For Tibetans, however, snow-capped mountains should not be climbed, but respected. They cannot be conquered because they are spirit mountains. Glacial ice is not to be walked on.

The Prince Temple is the largest temple on Kawagebo. Because the mountain is a prince, the temple is named after the mountain. One arrives at the temple through forest.

But upon arriving at this small clearing in the alpine, at first sight, I did not see the temple. A manidui stood centered in my path. I circumambulated the manidui clockwise, then walked toward the horses. As my pony stepped from the alpine shadows, I saw white — a glacier spreading up the side of Kawagebo. The Prince Temple was framed against white snow.

White overwhelmed my mind like the calling of wolves on a high Tibetan plateau at night when they go hungry and it is cold. I could hear their hunger and see the snow as a spirit calling in silence. Passing unwitting horses that were grazing on their own and resting between caravan loads, I realized they were surrounded by orange flowers, growing wildly on both sides of the pathway. I arrived at the Prince Temple walking through orange.

There was an old man waiting for us at the temple entrance. He was tending the temple. Suddenly, it occurred to me that maybe he had been here for years, from lifetime to lifetime. The thought flashed through my mind like sun hitting glacier snows at a point some time shortly after noon, when gold reflections persuade one's senses into believing that snow is the purest possession on earth. If you reach out to grab a handful of white, it melts.

I asked the old man how long he had been there. He told me thirteen years had already passed. He would continue to stay in the temple after I leave and wait there until he died. The next time I returned to the Kawagebo Mountain, he may not be there. He told me not to be bothered by this, or even to bother looking for him at that time, because it has not yet arrived, it is far more important to focus on that which has arrived at this moment of time.

The old man had no teeth, except maybe two, and was blind in one eye. I asked him why he chose to take care of the temple. He looked at me with one blind eye and said nothing. All I understood was that he planned to stay here, at the temple, sweeping the doorway for the rest of his life.

People would come and go, seeking something to bring back from the mountain. Maybe they would find it, maybe not. If they came with something, maybe they would not leave it behind. If they brought back something, then they were not empty. They had forgotten to take what was not there, or leave what had not been taken. So while waiting for pilgrims to come and go, the old man was pleased to tend the temple, but not point the way. Unbothered by pilgrims, he had already become part of the mountain.

Within the space of that moment, his life unfolded before me. Born a serf, he once had a landlord. His crime was loyalty to a landlord, who was purged after the Chinese revolution. He followed the Dalai Lama and left China for India, and lived a life among others who were poorer than him. He conducted some small businesses in India, apparently running a shop, tinkering with change. His ambition in life throughout the entirety of those years in India was to return to Yunnan, to the Kawagebo Mountain.

At that time, India and China did not have diplomatic relations. When conditions changed, he finally returned to Minyong, the village at the base of Kawagebo. There are only six shops in Minyong. For a toothless and half-blind old man in his late seventies, who was a former serf, there was nothing for him to do in Minyong, as the six shops vigorously compete for the small change of pilgrims and tourists coming and leaving Kawagebo. So instead of waiting for the pilgrims, he climbed the mountain, sleeping on the floor of the Prince Temple every night, caring for the images of the Buddha within.

It was at this point, the old man reminded me, that my pilgrimage up the mountain had not yet complete. The Prince Temple was only halfway up the mountain. Here, horse caravans stop, as the road beyond is thin and winding, hooves less sure where rivers crack at points where ice melts. But these are the points one must find, he explained. This was the entire purpose of climbing the mountain, if I wanted to find such points, the pilgrimage must be complete. This would mean climbing all the way up the mountain.

He said I could find this point at a place called the Lotus Temple,

the last point where the trail up the mountain ends. With a whisper of assurance, he explained that the further one climbs, the less one must climb. Climbing then becomes easier. Everything ends at the point where one can climb no more.

This old man's entire life was now devoted to a single purpose — looking after the temple. In fact, his only desire was to wait for the moment after I leave the temple. At that moment, nobody would be there to bother him. He could then continue to sweep the temple.

Conversation with a Stone

"The prince could see nothing in it at first except a mere stone, but the artist bade him' have a wall built, and make a window in it, and observe the stone through the window in the glory of dawn.' The prince did so, and then perceived that the stone was indeed very beautiful."

—*Lost Horizon*

CONVERSATION
with a stone

Walking clockwise behind the Prince Temple, the trail continues. Directly behind the temple, the trail passes a stone. It is an upright stone. The first impression is phallic, something like a linga one might see in India or Nepal. But it is a natural stone. It stands centered in the middle of the trail. To follow the trail, you must walk around the stone.

Tibetans believe this stone contains all the secrets of the earth, which will one day be told to those who learn to communicate with the stone. If you begin to understand this form of disintegrated logic, then you can begin trying to communicate with the stone.

But how does one begin to have a conversation with a stone? The conversation will begin at a point of disconnection. When everything is broken, you can begin trying to have a conversation with the stone. He will ignore you at first and say nothing. This does not mean that you should stand up, become frustrated and angry, and walk away. Do not start an argument with the stone. This would defeat the entire purpose of climbing Kawagebo.

Patience is needed, In some ways more than patience. You will require a vast sea of inner calm to keep your chakras in line and not to become unbalanced by the frustration of waiting.

When you wonder, how far to the top of the mountain do we have to go? You are already showing your frustration. Do not allow yourself to become off-centered. The ravens will become irritated by your anger. If you try to rant and rave, they

will laugh, and you, in turn, will become fragmented and even angrier, maybe even begin throwing stones at ravens. That will upset everybody. Then they will fly away in all directions and there will be no conclusion. This will leave more confusion than before you started trying to have a conversation with the stone. In such a case, it may be better to not even begin.

You will become distracted. People passing this way will look at you as if you have lost your mind. They may ask, what's the whole point of trying to speak with this rock? If you try to explain, they will tell you that they have had enough of your bullshit, and pass on. Let them go.

Sit in front of the stone cross-legged like attending a yoga class. Forget about the yogi and how much he charges per hour for the class,

or what time you need to be back at work after the class or the traffic conditions on the way, or the pop songs, commercials and weather report you may hear in the taxi waiting, stuck in traffic. Instead, stare at the stone. Listen to hints of what it might want to say.

Remember, the secrets of the earth understood by a silent stone cannot be transcendentally passed to others through either a mobile phone or an e-mail message. This impasse in technological development is crucial to understanding. As it means, there is no other way to communicate with a stone, except to sit cross-legged as if in yoga class and stare at your shadow as it stretches toward infinity. Then stare at the stone. Breathe as if meditating and face it until it ceases to become a stone in your mind for the space of a sequence between breaths. The sound of concentration is represented by the silence of time passing, which can extend for the entire contextual life of a stone, which means you have not been sitting here very long. Do not ask the stone too many personal questions. Just listen.

By listening, you will become aware of the sound of your own disintegration. Every second you remain on this earth in the form of meat and bone, the meat and bone will gradually be disintegrating until you realize that even your own presence ceases to exist. Then your shadow will disappear as well. Everything will be gone, including the credit cards. They too, will expire, and blow away. Eventually, the stone will be left by itself, without anybody to talk with. At the beginning of the process of ceasing to continue, you may begin to have a conversation with the stone.

If you both get along, then maybe when the time is right, it will share the secrets of the earth with you as well. This however, requires discarding your logical side of thinking, which forbids you from having a conversation with a stone. Such logic can be easily removed from the backpack of your life and tossed into the ravine running nearby the temple. The backpack will feel lighter and walking becomes easier. This is because the discarded items have fallen into the ravine, which leads nowhere in particular except back down the mountain.

The ravine was cut by the purity of glacial ice melting to become a river. So it is a good place to discard logic. Ultimately, logic will drive you to find the point where ice melts. This is where the river begins. But you cannot find it so easily. Especially if you begin looking for logic already discarded from your backpack. It can no longer be found, having dissipated in the river.

So don't try to follow the logic. It will lead you down the river back to the bottom of the mountain. Instead, look for the glacier.It is the source of the river. It is the place where water and ice begin to disconnect."

Conversation with a Dakini

"Conway went to the balcony and gazed at the dazzling plume of Karakal; the moon was riding high in a waveless ocean. It came to him that a dream had dissolved, like all too lovely things, at the first touch of reality; that the whole world's future, weighed in the balance against youth and love, would be light as air."

—*Lost Horizon*

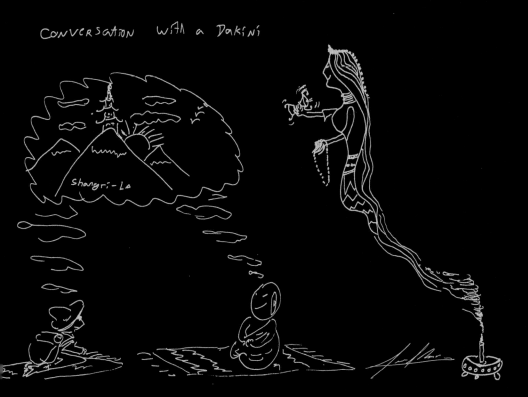

Walking into the forest shadows led along the trail continuing behind the Prince Temple. The trail led to an opening in the forest, a small field surrounded by prayer flags. The grass was dried and I noticed some places where the earth was raw and exposed.

Pilgrims climbing Kawagebo will bring ashes from the bones of dead relatives, and dust the ashes here, leaving them spread everywhere across the dried grass. Then, the pilgrims themselves will roll over the ashes spread upon this spot. It feels like a raw wound cut into the earth. Afterwards they stand up, and dust their ashes into wind, which blows them everywhere.

The anxiety of rolling upon the ashes, spread upon this place, of those you have loved, is the fullest expression that we too have all died once already, and are now living a new life. In the end, we begin a new cycle.

Deeper in the forest, I crossed another stream that led to what local Tibetans claimed were the dancing grounds of Dakinis, divine female spirits, something like angels. They have not yet become Bodhisattvas because their presence on earth cannot be felt long enough to hold them. You may have seen their images painted on the ceilings of Tang Dynasty caves in Dunhuang along the Silk Road. They are always depicted dancing Some dance as they fly because they cannot descend to earth long enough to be present.

On the open grassland it is said that they dance around trees and rocks at night when nobody is looking. They can drive you crazy like a lover, or lead you in a direction to find what you were looking for. Sometimes, they are clearer than you about what you want. Sometimes, they are totally confused and leave you searching in frustration, chasing their shadows without any hope of conclusion. This is the function of Dakinis. They lead you to find yourself by leading you to follow and chase them, in imprecise directions.

Here at this grassy spot in the center of Kawagebo's ancient cedar forest, where Dakinis are supposed to descend to dance and sing, prayer flags have been placed by Tibetan pilgrims around trees and rocks. The pilgrims visit this place during the day, so as not to disturb the Dakinis,

knowing they dance at night when nobody is there to listen.

They danced in this place because Padmasambhava, the Lotus-Born Master practiced tantric rituals in a stone cave on a flat cliff above the trees. The Lotus-Born Master did not chase the Dakinis because he was too busy meditating with them.

To find the place he meditated, enter the trees, climb a cliff, grabbing roots hung like handles on a public bus, pulling a rope strung there for assisting pilgrims who might come to meditate in the Lotus-Born Master's cave. After pulling on roots and ropes, you will find the cave. But this cave is really not a cave at all but a half-open crevice in the cliff, a cave with half a roof, a cave that might have once been a cave before it caved in. The space within the smooth rock was equally round on all sides, a perfect place to meditate while listening to the

sound of the river tumbling across rocks below.

From this retreat of Padmasambhava, the Lotus-Born Master, one can hear the river, but watching white water may be difficult. Branches grow across the entrance. Space through which one can look outside is reduced by the shady brilliance of green leaves.

So if you wish to concentrate on space while meditating, look up at the ridges of the mountains touching the sky. So rather than meditating by looking down at the earth in front, the Lotus-Born Master must have meditated on the sky.

As I sat in the cave listening to the river, I began to understand why Padmasambhava, the Lotus-Born Master had come to Kawagebo. I also understood why the sound of blue is green.

Behind the cave on the cliff is another cliff. It can be reached by grabbing onto roots and ropes others have left behind to find the sacred waterfall, where water trickles in delicate shower-like spray.

The water from this rock, behind the place where Padmasambhava, the Lotus-Born Master meditated, purifies. It is said to have the same powers as water from Yuepeng, the most sacred of springs on Kawagebo. It purifies all evils in an individual. I bathed in the water, and then drank it. It tasted cold. It tasted like melting glaciers.

Further up the train past another large manidui is the place is called "Kha Zhu Mayi Tsu Yang". The manidui is built upon a natural stone bowl said to have once been used to place vinegar, the food eaten by Dakinis.

Local Tibetan pilgrims warned about feeding the Dakinis. Dakinis usually appear as charmed young girls flying and dancing. Some carry musical instruments. They can bring your wishes to the deities, serving as intermediaries or mediums with both universes, and tap into your hidden spiritual wealth, helping you accomplish tasks if your intention is positive. But if your intention is wrong, they will deliberately make a mess out of everything. Then there is nothing you can do about it. So do not try to feed the Dakinis or call upon them unless you are absolutely sure about what you are doing."

Dakinis can be understood as energy forces that can pierce time zones, travel through space, interacting with other galaxies and planetary movements. They represent subtle, untapped knowledge inside your body. They can fly anywhere, any place, at any time. They know no seasons. Colors change into a spectrum with just a blink of an eye. When you blink, a Dakini may have arrived, or gone. Their interaction with space is fluid. That is why they hide among echoes between the ancient cedar trees in the mountains. Like the mountains, they serve to connect between earth and heaven.

If someone needs the help of a Dakini, they can be summoned through a lama using a hand-held drum. In ancient times, the drums were made from a pair of adolescent skull craniums of a boy and a girl, representing unity of two pure souls. When shaken briskly the rat-tat-tat-tat summons the Dakinis, just like that. When summoning Dakinis, remember that like charmed young girls, careful management is very necessary. Assistance of a skilled lama is highly recommended to maintain control over the situation. Remember, Dakinis can appear where you least expect them. By looking, you can never find them. They arrive when you have no expectations. When you expect them to arrive, they leave.

Reaching the Glaciers

"But the feeling was only momentary, and soon merged in
the deeper sensation, half mystical, half visual, of having
reached at last some place that was an end, a finality."

—Lost Horizon

Reaching the Glaciers

Prayer flags between pine trees were across a place where wind would carry prayers to the mountain peak and beyond. Tibetans say the horses' heads printed on each prayer flag must face the mountain. The horses will continue the journey we have begun by riding the wind. This is the point of connectivity between mountain and sky, where Dakinis come to dance, the valley of the glacier, the place where echoes hide I looked at the prayer flag and was certain that the direction of the horse's head had changed. That is the direction thoughts will blow when the wind shifts. It reminds us to return to the mountain one day in our subconscious at a point to be arrived at, only when we finally cease to remember.

The pilgrims who came all carried burdens on their backs, sometimes in backpacks, sometimes without. All of us spend our entire lives carrying burdens, sometimes knowingly, sometimes not. Like scars on our body, they weigh on our back, tattoos on our minds. We

cannot live without them. We have all come this way before without really knowing or asking why, maybe in this lifetime, maybe the next. The difference can be discovered in the deliberateness of arrival and departure. To leave a place like this without the burdens brought, with only complete emptiness, may be the most difficult task of all.

As one approaches the glaciers of Kawagebo, there is a place where moss covers trees as thick as grass and air is cool, kept moist by glaciers. This is where one finds the Lotus Temple The central image in the Lotus Temple is Padmasambhava, the Lotus-Born Master himself.Legend says that Padmasambhava was discovered as a baby sitting upon a lotus, a miraculous birth. The lotus is a core symbol in Buddhism. The roots of a lotus are immersed deep into mud amidst stagnant water. The lotus stem grows out from the mud and rises above seeking the light, spreading its radiant purple or pink flower toward the sun. In many ways Buddhism teaches us to be like the lotus.

We need to rise above the muck and seek clarity somewhere above. Sometimes we have to go through a lot of muck before we can get there.

Upon entering the temple complex, my thoughts were then shattered by a ring, which brought the glass panels of my mind crashing into a thunderous rampage as if a water pipe had burst, ripping out the big thick glass window panes of a five-star hotel lobby. When the last piece of glass fell to the marble floor like a pin dropping into a canyon, it suddenly occurred to me that I was receiving a call on my mobile phone, which had no connection in the valleys, but now stuck me with shock near the glacier line.

I answered. A voice called, "Hey brother!" It was David Garcia, a high-flying steel commodity trader and jet-set investor from Hong Kong. He wanted to discuss his steel factory in Nanjing. I had helped him set it up when working as a lawyer before I quit my profession. He now wanted to sell it, divest, and get out of the China market. The question was how to structure the legal aspects of this divestment deconstruction while arranging foreign exchange repatriation without losing on the forward market. He needed divestment advice with a complicated analysis of the risks and returns within virtual time, there — before the open doors of the Lotus Temple.

"David, I am now at the entrance to the Lotus Temple at the highest point of one of the most sacred Tibetan mountains," my voice stuttered, "which means I have reached the most conscious point of consciousness," I tried to explain myself. "So can a decision on this transaction wait long enough for the Tibetan sitting cross-legged beside me to finish carving 'Om Mani Bemi Hom' on a stone to be left behind on the mountain as a prayer when I leave the mountain? Have you ever heard of the mantra 'Om Mani Bemi Hom'?"

"Of course," David snapped back. "I'm from Laguna Beach. In the 1960s, you couldn't get laid without reciting 'Om Mani Bemi Hom' to the chicks on the beach."

Suddenly, I realized that even on a sacred mountain one could not get away from the ringing of a mobile phone. This point pierced my mind like fact.

Buddhists say one may become enlightened at strange and unpredictable moments. Sometimes, it has nothing to do with meditating or sitting in a forest listening to the sound of one hand clapping. Sometimes, it happens when you are not there to hear a

branch fall. Sometimes, it happens when you are standing before the entrance of the Lotus Temple looking out upon the glaciers of Kawagebo, and then a mobile phone rings.

I hung up the phone. The transaction dissipated into an electromagnetic wave that drifted somewhere precariously without direction. I decided to sit cross-legged on the floor before yak butter candles that were burning. A glow emanated throughout the space around me. In the darkness the caretaker sat. He rose and moved into the flickering light of butter candles. Feeling my confusion, he told me the riddle of how this temple came to be.

It was the story of an Indian yogi who had come to Kawagebo centuries ago. After meditating for seven days, he found a yellow cow sleeping on a space of grass on a mountain slope. "Why was there such a clean space of grass on the side of such a steep mountain slope?" the yogi asked. "Why did a yellow cow choose to sleep there by itself?"

There was nobody tending the cow, no farmhouse, no roads, not one single person. So the cow belonged to no one. The Indian teacher went over to look at it. But when he reached it, the cow disappeared, leaving behind only a pile of manure. There was no other trace of its presence. When the Indian teacher tried to clean up the mess, he discovered a golden statue of Buddha inside. Intuitively, he built the temple here to mark the spot.

The yogi then sent a stray cat into a nearby cave. According to local Tibetans, the cave leads straight through Kawagebo to India. The cat brought a message back to India that the temple was built by the yogi. So the yogi sent his message in real time even without digital communications. The stray cat was the precursor to the Internet. I wondered how many stray cats are running through our minds with similar messages, and whether we really need the Internet to send them.

The Lotus Temple stands as a lotus shaped silhouette before ice creeping down from clouds beneath glaciers tumbling across rocks. Following the manidui stones clockwise around the temple, one reaches the back of the temple where the trail continued clockwise to the front. But must eventually, after encircling the temple, go back down the mountain. The journey returns to where you came from. The point of arrival is also the point of departure.

Behind the temple where the trail curves, a vast precipice valley separated space of the temple's golden roof arches, from the precipice of glaciers. This is the point behind the Lotus Temple where you cannot go any further. Face the snows. They will tell you, this is as far as you can go. But do not let perceptions dissuade our senses, because we can always go further.

Speaking to the mountain, you can hear voices echo, the sound of snow melting, drowned by the soprano voice of a raven laughing across the precipice. Rows of prayer flags drawn between pine trees, tied by pilgrims who came here before, and left. Afterwards, the raven laughs again, then flies away.

Here, space between dissipating clouds and mountain snows is empty. Water melting from glaciers, tumbling across rocks, is the sound of fear being released from one's mind. The sound of rolling clouds can be heard against the echo of snow. Like meditation, it is a state of emptiness to be brought from the place where you were meditating, upon finishing and leaving that place. I tried to recall the journey that had brought me to this place.

I tried to remember. Before glacial snows, childhood images returned. Standing on Kawagebo, I could not get them out of my mind. Once again, I wondered what it would be like to live in a timber house on a mountainside with nothing else around except wild flowers floating in wind and the sound of one's own echo dreamily calling out from within in the depths of a chasm that cut through terraced fields by a river flowing from melting glaciers in mountains, which can never be climbed. I thought about climbing such a mountain. It was the sound of clouds departed.

Conclusion

"We sat for a long time in silence, and then talked again
of Conway as I remembered him...and the strange ultimate
dream of Blue Moon. 'Do you think he will ever find it?' I
asked."

—Lost Horizon.

A pilgrimage to any sacred mountain, on any continent, can be understood as a journey that takes place on many different levels at once.

To begin, a pilgrimage is a trip to a holy place. But on another level, each pilgrimage isa journey to one's own self. By seeking a destination, we must dump out the accumulated burdens in our own packpack. The journey then becomes lighter. Only by clearing the static, can we explore our own subconscious. In the forgotten cognizant spaces of our mind, which are vast and unending, answers to all things can be found. They exist there, and have only been waiting for us to find the key to open the compartments. So we can think of the destination in a pilgrimage journey as representing a spacial construct of our mind is a microcosom of the universe. The pilgrimage, is simply the route we take to get there.

Trekking the Tea Caravan Trail in 2003 was more than an expedition, matching the places described in Hilton's "Lost Horizon" with actual locations in Yunnan Province. The journey would change the

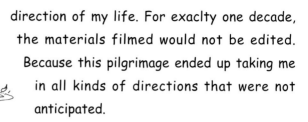

direction of my life. For exaclty one decade, the materials filmed would not be edited. Because this pilgrimage ended up taking me in all kinds of directions that were not anticipated.

The trek revealed a sharp juxtaposition between two sets of values. On one hand there was the brand and money worship that had engulfed most Chinese cities. The notion of "globalization" had reached a peak in 2003. Our mainstream media dared not to even question whether our entire planet should not become one modular shopping mall. But every step on this journey along the Tea Caravan Trail, challenged this assumption, and the mainstream view.

Returning to Beijing shortly after the filming, I had a real problem putting on my suit and tie again. Feeling new alignment in hiking boots and torn jeans, I met a lama and began meditating. Within two years I would leave the Mercedes, BMW and Ferrari choked streets of Beijing, move to Lhasa, and begin work pioneering a social enterprise. From there, the work of developing a social enterprise would connect with the experiences of others across the Himalayan region. Soon, I would go everywhere.

The Himalayan Consensus as an economic paradigm would evolve from the collective efforts of many people seeking a more holistic way of managing both our lives and economies while protecting culture and the environment. This idea would spread to other continents and connect with like-minded thoughts and actions occurring across the globe. The African Consensus would arise. So would a Barcelona Consensus and a Russian Consensus as well. Occupy Wall Street would follow, and become Occupy Everywhere.

I would spend the years ahead taking alternative approaches to economics, connecting the constellation of movements across continents, and pointing out that it had become a new mainstream. People wanting change have taken action into their own hands, and at the community level they are making things better for themselves and their children. The mainstream media ignore it. And the politicians keep talking. That is why they are unable to listen.

Separate and independent movements, these progressive community efforts across our global all share common values of prioritizing our environment, and using our global resources in a more equitable and sustainable manner. Ideals of diversified localization rather than monolithic globalization are at the core of this movement. As different spokes of global progressive economics, these independent yet interconnected efforts call for empowerment of people through compassionate capital at the community level and conscientious consumption to change the behavior of corporations.

From one journey, many new ones begin.By sharing one experience, many new ones arise. Thank you for joining me on this journey. I have felt your presence the entire way. As it ends, now please begin your own journey.

It starts by having a conversation with a sacred mountain.

AFTERWORD

In 2003, I trekked the ancient "tea caravan trail" in northern Yunnan Province following Hilton's classic novel "Lost Horizon" in which he described Shangri-la. Indigenous people along the trail each have their own sacred mountain that protects them. It is a dialogue that teaches us the importance of preserving our natural environment that will in turn assure our existence.

Between 2002-2005, I led three expeditions in search of Shangri-la. Each became both an experimental documentary film and a book.

The style is called "doc-fiction." Actual scenes are filmed spontaneously as in a documentary. However, we use a story line to link events. The books are written in the same style. Events are linked with a story. That's why we call it "doc-fiction."

Sometimes we need a story to bring us on a journey that we were always meant to go on but would not have taken the first step without that urge to search for something that maybe we cannot ever find. Sometimes a journey is more important than arriving at the final destination.

I never found Shangri-la. But along the way I met many people of

different ethnic backgrounds determined to protect their culture and environment. In many ways they were creating their own Shangri-la. I thank them, because they changed the way I think.

They established micro-businesses to sustain culture and protect their own ethnicity. The concept of social enterprise arose from their experiences. Inspired by them, in 2005 I moved to Lhasa and established Shambhala Serai, a social enterprise that protects heritage architecture, and supports medical, education, and nomadic outreach programs.

I hope you enjoy my story. More important, I hope it inspires you to live your own life differently from what others expect or want you to do. Don't listen to those who want to stop you. Just pursue your own journey, and go all the way, wherever it leads.

Always trust your instincts. They are never wrong.

And always remember, a single idea can take you in all kinds directions that you never expected.

So if you have an idea, just pursue it.

Searching for Shangri-la
Can You Find It?

As the 21st Century dawned, in the year 2000, a debate arose in western China among different regions each claiming to be the historical location of Shangri-la. Cities like Dali, Lijiang, and Zhongdian, vied with Lhasa, Yushu and Xiahe for the designation, all claiming to be the original Shangri-la.

Ironically, there was no higher motivation in competing for the title, other than luring tourist dollars.

Nevertheless, the question had finally been put on the table: Where is the real Shangri-la?

It sparked author and environmentalist Laurence Brahm to launch the Searching for Shangri-la Expeditions Project.

The Shangri-la Expeditions Project

The Searching for Shangri-la Project sought to understand the source of the Shangri-la myth and whether it could actually be associated with a single location in Western China.

Throughout the first decade of the 21st Century, Searching for Shangri-la Expeditions Project launched three major expeditions to find out the geographical location of Shangri-la.

The Project was determined to discover the origins rooted behind the myth.

Three Expeditions Become the Himalayan Trilogy

In 2017, the trilogy of books about the three expeditions: Searching for Shangri-la, Conversations with Sacred Mountains, Shambhala Sutra, have been published by IBIS, the leading American new age publishing house, to raise awareness of environmental concerns and those of our own subconscious.

The first Searching for Shangri-la expedition launched from Lhasa in 2002 went north to Qinghai, before tracking south through Yunnan Province. Throughout this expedition, the Searching for Shangri-la team pursued one single inquiry: where is Shangri-la? The first book in the Himalayan Trilogy, Searching for Shangri-la, is based on notes from this expedition. After searching everywhere and conducting countless field interviews, the expedition team determined that Shangri-la could not be found.

However, the expedition revealed that Shangri-la was first described in James Hilton's novel Lost Horizon, published in 1933. Shangri-la captured the Western imagination in the 1930s during the Great Depression when all faith in capital markets and financial materialism was lost. So people turned to loftier ideals of spiritualism, as exemplified by Shangri-la. Due to its popularity, Lost Horizon became one of the first Hollywood movies.

Regrouping in 2003, the Searching for Shangri-la expedition team conducted detailed research and analysis of Lost Horizon. They found: historically, James Hilton never visited Asia. He certainly never visited the Himalayas, nor even Tibet for that matter. Hilton apparently based all of his writing on reports from Joseph Rock, National Geographic's first Bureau Chief in China, based in Yunnan Province.

In 2003, the Searching for Shangri-la expedition team followed the footsteps of Joseph Rock along the Tea Caravan Trail that for centuries had served as the main route for transporting Pu'er tea from Yunnan overland to Lhasa, and on to India. On the return journey back from India, pony caravans carried Buddhist sutra. Historically the Tea Caravan Trail was a vital route for Buddhist philosophy entering China. The second book in the Himalayan Trilogy, Conversations with Sacred Mountains, is based on notes from this second expedition.

During the expedition, it was discovered that "Shangri-la" is actually a misspelling of the word "Shambhala," an ideal realm in Tibetan Buddhism.

A new question arose: How to find Shambhala?

By 2004 the search for Shambhala had been launched. The Searching for Shangri-la team had discovered a rare ancient text hidden at Tashilumpu Monastery in Shigatze, central Tibet. Could it offer clues? Written in the 1700s by the Sixth Panchen Lama, the sutra serves as a travel guidebook offering physical locations that could possibly guide one to the mysterious realm of Shambhala. The third book in the Himalayan Trilogy, Shambhala Sutra, is based on notes from this third expedition.

The Searching for Shangri-la expedition soon discovered that the coordinates described in the sutra could not be found on GPS.

Following the Sutra's designations, the expedition crossed Ngari Prefecture, the most isolated and inaccessible part of western Tibet, arriving upon the ancient abandoned city of Guge, rising out of the desert like a ghost city. Could this be Shambhala?

After thorough archeological investigation the expedition team determined that Guge is not Shambhala.

So then where does one go to find Shambhala? Moreover, what is it?

The Shambhala Prophecy—Oracle of Our Age

The Shambhala Sutra text reveals a prophecy: 2500 years after the Nirvana of the historical Buddha Lord Shakyamuni, the world will be in the Age of Kali, or self-destruction. Mankind driven by an ideology of greed and shortsighted profit will destroy his own environment through blind economic growth, and exploitative principles that enrich an elite and impoverish the rest. The Shambhala Sutra predicts that in the Age of Kali karmic revenge manifests itself through natural catastrophe, new diseases that cannot be cured, cycles of wars, conflict and terror, all specifically described in the sutra.

In the Kingdom of Shambhala, everything is harmonious, people respect nature and there are no prejudices. Those who have give to those who don't. Principles of equality, environmental protection and peace are the philosophy of all twenty-five kings who reign in succession for periods of one hundred years each. Kalachakra tantra is the core teaching of the Shambhala Kings.

The Kings of Shambhala look down, observing this mess. Finally, dismayed by the situation on earth, the last King of Shambhala dispatches the warriors of Shambhala to rid our universe of the demonic forces of greed, anger and ignorance, that are defined by Buddhism as "the three poisons." Fossil fuels are outlawed and the trading of derivatives regulated. The King of Shambhala then heralds a new era of peace, harmony, ecological civilization, and mutual respect within the community of mankind.

According to the legend explained in the sutra, our future is Shambhala, sometimes misspelled as "Shangri-la."

But how do we get there? Try the power of intention.

Searching for Shangri-la—The Exhibition

In 2016, National Geographic Air and Water and Conservation Fund Award recognized the Searching for Shangri-la Expeditions Project for its contribution in raising awareness of the impending water and ecological crisis our planet faces.

The award was applied to present a major exhibition of the three expeditions across the Himalayan region of western China, in search of the mythical land called Shangri-la, to raise social awareness of ecological and water conservation concerns.

The source materials for the artistic work derive from drawings, video and photo documentation captured during three Searching for Shangri-la expeditions that were conducted during the first decade of the 21st Century, searching for the lost kingdom of Shangri-la. In many respects the exhibition is a multi-media and multi-dimensional presentation of the

Himalayan Trilogy, which as installation art carries the audience as participants along this incredible journey, in the end unlocking mysteries of Shangri-la in their own subconscious.

The exhibition was first displayed in Autumn 2016 at Three Shadows Photography and Art Center in Beijing, the penultimate cinematography and photography museum founded by Chinese avant guard photographer Rong Rong and designed by Ai Weiwei. The exhibition will travel to other parts of Asia, Europe and the United States alongside publication of the Himalayan Trilogy by IBIS Press.

Laurence Brahm
explorer, author, environmentalist:

As an international crisis mediation lawyer and developmental economist, Laurence Brahm's concerns over climate disruption and impending global water crisis led him to launch the Searching for Shangri-la Expeditions Project at the beginning of this century. As explorer, film director and documentarian of the Searching for Shangri-la Expeditions, he spent over a decade in remote regions of the Tibetan plateau producing film documentaries and the Himalayan Trilogy of books, for which he was elected a Fellow International of the Explorer's Club of New York in 2015.

Inspired by the Shambhala story, he was determined to put intention into action, and established Shambhala Serai as one of Asia's first social enterprises that involved heritage restoration, identity empowerment, through establishing a chain of heritage lodges in Tibet. These lodges are entirely run and managed by local Tibetans and energized with solar power, and have in turn supported through their operation the establishment of medical clinics for rural and nomadic communities, a rural school with Montessori education programs, vocational training for Tibetans suffering from disabilities and three thousand operations to cure blindness in nomadic regions. Forbes Magazine featured the social enterprise in January 2016 as being one of the earliest social enterprises in Asia. Further, in June 2016, the Pontifical Council for Peace and Justice at the Vatican Impact Investing Conference recognized Laurence Brahm's work as exemplifying "Successful Social Enterprise."

The idea of expanding social enterprise values to all corporations underlay his vision to found the Himalayan Consensus Institute. From 2014, the Himalayan Consensus Summit began convening in Kathmandu as an annual dialogue between environmentalists, business finance leaders in proposing policy recommendations to regional governments to address poverty alleviation, community empowerment, and the threats of anthropomorphic climate disruption. The Himalayan Consensus process is now viewed by both governments and environmental Institutions in Asia as offering a second track dialogue toward preventing crisis and conflict over precious water resources in Asia.

In 2015 Iceland's President Olafur Ragnar Grimsson invited him to serve on the Himalaya – Third Pole Circle, a panel forming policy responses to glacial melt caused by climate change. That same year he was invited to serve on ICIMOD's Hindu Kush Himalaya Assessment Monitoring Panel, and to advise Bhutan's National Environment Commission on waste and cyclical economics.

Laurence Brahm spearheaded drafting of China's Ecological Civilization Policy for transformation of energy grids from fossil fuels to renewable sources. Between 2013-2015, as senior advisor to China's Minister of Environmental Protection, he simultaneously served as advisor to the European Commission Director General on Environment, and coordinated advice between the European Commission, World Wildlife Fund, China's scientists and policymakers in drafting the Ecological Civilization Opinion document that became the keystone of China's national policy on environment adopted by the State Council and Central Committee on April 25, 2015. In this respect, the Searching for Shangri-la expeditions project inspired the Himalayan Consensus dialogue process that in turn contributed to China's Ecological Civilization policy. For this reason in 2016, National Geographic Society recognized the importance of the Searching for Shangri-la expeditions through the National Geographic Air and Water Conservation Fund award. In 2016 he received China's national Social Responsibility Award at Diao Yutai State Guest House together with celebrity pianist Lang Lang. On this occasion he was formally recognized as "the earliest articulator of the ecological civilization concept" and the father of China's environmental policy. It was the first time a foreigner has received China's highest national award for social responsibility.

In 2012 he served as NGO spokesperson to the United Nations Earth Summit 2012 (Rio+20), and was selected by ScenaRio as one of the "100 Opinion Leaders Advising Rio+20". In 2010 he received the UNDP Award for Bio-Diversity and Cultural Protection in China presented by Jane Goodall. In 2009 China's Central Television recognized him as "One of the ten individuals contributing to China's reform and opening" and the only foreigner among the ten. In 2008 United National Secretary General Pan Ki-Moon personally visited his courtyard heritage home in Beijing inviting him to join the United Nations Theme Group for Poverty and Inequality. He has authored over thirty books on Asian economics, politics, culture and heritage.

The Himalayan Trilogy Series

The three expeditions undertaken by explorer, author, and environmentalist Laurence J. Brahm between 2002 and 2004. Brahm discovers that the beauty and silence of the mountain passes, rivers, and great valleys mirror the interior state of his soul, and that the future of humanity depends on our being able to modify our own economies and cultures to be more in harmony with our planet.

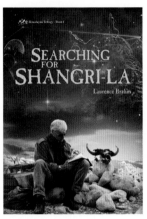

Trim: 6.125 x 9
Page count: 272 pages
Full Color
Price: $22.95
Sewn softcover
Book ISBN:
978-0-89254-220-8
Ebook ISBN:
978-0-89254-635-0

Searching for Shangri-la
Off the Beaten Track in Western China
(Book I)

In 2002, Laurence J. Brahm, inspired by James Hilton's novel Lost Horizon and his own quest for meaning, began his search for Shangri-la. Some say that Shangri-la can be found in sacred Tibet, or maybe in wild Qinghai; others believe it can be found in artistic Yunnan in the southwest of China. The author discovered the spiritual truth that Shangri-la is not a place. Rather it is a state of mind.

The myth of Shangri-la has become a source of creative inspiration for many people, drawing China's leading figures in pop culture and art circles to western China, all in search of understanding. In this fascinating book, we meet many of China's leading cultural figures: such as composer San Bao, dancer Yang Liping, pop singer Dadawa, together with other artists, lamas, and living Buddhas.

Searching for Shangri-la is the first book of the Himalayan Trilogy. The reader will discover the need for fresh economic paradigms that call for compassionate capital, empowering people, and prioritizing the environment. Spirituality can be more powerful than materialism. The need for sustainability has rarely been so beautifully and eloquently defended. Brahm and his fellow seekers issue a clarion call for the protection of our environment and the values of culture and spirituality, the embrace of an alternate philosophy whose planetary and ethnic consequences will bring a renewal of hope and joy.

Conversations with Sacred Mountains
A Journey Along Yunnan's Tea Caravan Trail
(Book II)

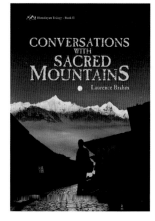

Laurence Brahm made his second journey in 2003. He followed the actual route of Lost Horizon along the ancient Tea Caravan Trail in Yunnan Province of southwest China.

Starting in the capital city of Kunming, he traveled from Dali to Lijiang to Lugo Lake, to Zhongdian and Deqin and the sacred Kawegabo Mountain. Each region has its own culture and ethnic tradition and is trying to preserve the old way of life while adapting to the economic realities of modern life and tourism.

What makes a mountain sacred? Laurence learns about the waning cultures of the ethnic minorities such as the Bai, the Dai, the Yi, the Naxi and the Mosu. He meets various individuals who share stories about the misty mountains that stand majestically in this land.

Trim: 6.125 x 9
Page count: 272 pages
Full Color
Price: $22.95
Sewn softcover
Book ISBN:
978-0-89254-221-5
Ebook ISBN:
978-0-89254-636-7

Shambhala Sutra
The Road Less Traveled in Western Tibet
(Book III)

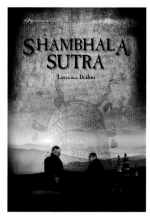

Following the Shambhala Sutra—an ancient manuscript written by Panchen Lama over two hundred ago—the author started his journey to Shambhala, traveling through the deserts and mountains in Tibet. The journey began in Lhasa and continued deep into the harsh regions of Tibet.

Brahm's 2004 expedition across western Tibet's Ngari region taught him that the ancient sutra was a metaphorical guidebook. Lessons learned from this journey are that short sighted greed, war and failure to protect our environment will cause kingdoms and empires to vanish. By bringing the peaceful positive energy into practice, you can help people and change the world. This is the genuine way to Shambhala.

Trim: 6.125 x 9
Page count: 272 pages
Full Color
Price: $22.95
Sewn softcover
Book ISBN:
978-0-89254-222-2
Ebook ISBN:
978-0-89254-637-4

Published in 2017 by Ibis Press
A division of Nicolas-Hays, Inc.
P. O. Box 540206
Lake Worth, FL 33454-0206
www.ibispress.net

Distributed to the trade by
Red Wheel/Weiser, LLC
65 Parker St. · Ste. 7
Newburyport, MA 01950
www.redwheelweiser.com

Isbn 978-089254-221-5
Ebook: Isbn 978-0-89254-636-7

Library of Congress Cataloging-in-Publication Data
Available Upon Request

Designer: Xie Jinbao
Book Production: Studio 31

Printed in China
[AP]

Please visit the author's website: HimalayanConsensus.org
and on YouTube: Laurence Brahm Channel
Searching for Shangri-la